Common Errors in English

Published by
Lotus Press Publishers & Distributors

Common Errors in English

M. Thomas

Lotus Press
4735/22, Prakash Deep Building,
Ansari Road, Daryaganj,
New Delhi - 110002

Lotus Press : Publishers & Distributors
Unit No. 220, 2nd Floor, 4735/22, Prakash Deep Building,
Ansari Road, Darya Ganj, New Delhi- 110002
Ph.: 23280047, 98118-38000
• E-mail : lotuspress1984@gmail.com
www.lotuspress.co.in

Common Errors in English

ISBN: 81-89093-91-6

Printed & Published by : **Lotus Press Publisher & Distributors,** New Delhi-02

Preface

English grammar is a complex topic. It is not easy, and one should be very careful while using it. There are common and uncommon errors that one commits while using the English language either in written or in spoken contexts.

This book has been written to analyse the various errors made in spoken and written English. It also gives explanations and guidelines to correct the common and uncommon errors.

There are certain principles of usage for English (or for that matter for any language) which are to be followed for the 'acceptable expression' of that language and this book aims to highlight those principles of usage.

There are certain 'relaxations' in using English. Relaxation refers to 'flexibility' in using certain aspects of the grammar. Rules are rigid in English grammar but at certain instances of usage, these rigid rules are relaxed to make the language easy and simple to comprehend.

The rules for usage are necessary to maintain the uniformity of meaning that language has had across the years. 'Guidelines for usage' are important for this purpose.

Most of the competitive examinations and recruitment agencies ask questions relating to common errors in the General English paper. This shows the immense importance of writing correct English, and in the case of interviews the importance of correct spoken English.

The importance of English, as an international language, is increasing day by day in this competitive world. Persons knowing English have an advantage over those who do not know it.

Similarly, persons using correct English have tremendous advantage over those who do not know the appropriate usage. One must use the English language in an accurate, lucid and appropriate manner in both speech and writing.

This book serves as a 'guide' to students, teachers, laymen and people in all walks of life, to speak and write correct English avoiding common and uncommon errors. Constructive suggestions are invited from the readers to improve this book and to include anything left out.

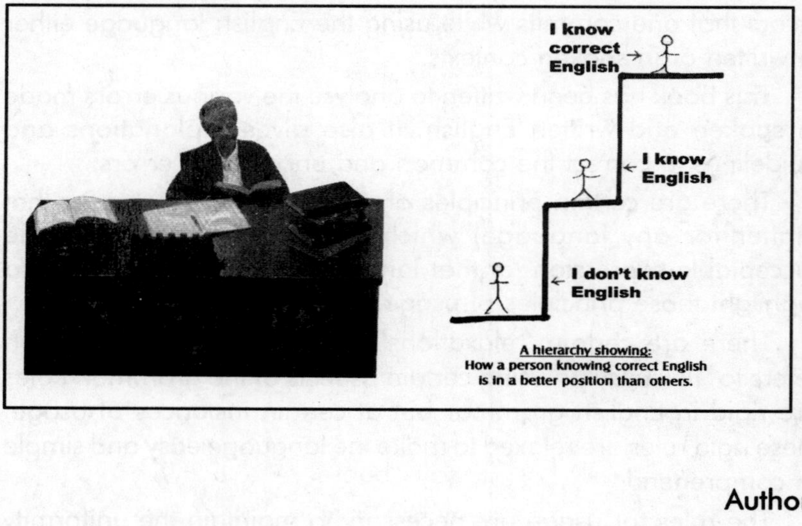

A hierarchy showing:
How a person knowing correct English is in a better position than others.

Author

PROLOGUE

The spelling of English is a pitfall for most of us at some time or another. The most common error in English is in the spelling of words. Here are some oddities for your amusement. Isn't English a wonderful language?

SOB STORY

Today, away from me you fly,
Though, yesterday, to me you flew,
So now I am disposed to cry,
Though here to fore I never crew.

NOT HARD TO SWALLOW

I wonder what would help me cough;
A cup of coughey should.
At least it would not bump me ough,
And it might do me gould.

THE POINT IS MOOT

If you say, 'boot',
Then why not 'foot'?
And on your feet,
You should wear beet.

COMPANION PEACE

A jug of wine beneath the bough
and milk from Yon contended cough
And you beside me makes me glow
Deliciously, from head to tow.

Margaret Fishback

The wind was rough
And cold and blough
She kept her hands inside her mough.
It chilled her through
Her nose turned blough
And still the squall the faster flough.
And yet although
There was no snough
The weather was a cruel fough.
It made her cough
(Please do not scough);
She coughed until her hat blew ough.

Bennett Cerf

Contents

1

ENGLISH—THE UNIVERSAL BINDER

Why this book on 'Common Errors' in English? This is a question in the minds of many people. The answer to their question lies in the following facts:

1. English is the most widespread language in the world, and is more widely spoken and written than any other language.
2. Over 400 million people use the English vocabulary as a mother tongue, only surpassed in numbers, by those who speak the varius forms of Chinese language.
3. 700 million people speak English as a foreign language.
4. Of all the world languages (over 2,700), English is arguably the richest in vocabulary; and it is that the *Oxford English Dictionary* lists about 500,000 words, and a further half million technical and scientific terms remain uncatalogued.
5. Three-quarters of the world's mail, telexes and cables are in English.
6. Five of the largest broadcasting companies in the world (CBS, NBC, ABC, BBC and CBC) speak in English, reaching millions and millions of people all over the world.
7. The main language used on the Internet is English.

8. More than half of the world's technical and scientific periodicals are in English.
9. English is the medium for 80 per cent of the information stored in the world's computers.
10. English is the language of navigation, aviation and of Christianity. It is the Ecumenical language of the World Council of Churches.

English is the most widespread language in the world, and is more widely spoken and written than any other language.

These facts highlight the importance of English as a spoken language, a medium of instruction, written and as a computer language. When we look at the merits of this language, we cannot ignore the various errors committed in the use of this language. As one finds out the various errors commonly encountered in the use of this language one wants to know how to correct them. If there is a poison, there is a corresponding antidote; similarly for every error there is a correction.

Errors in English can be both common and uncommon. If there is a scribble, there is also calligraphy. Similarly at one end of the spectrum, you have errors in English and at the other end is the highly refined, grammatically perfect English with 100 per cent clarity in diction, thoughts and expression. When embarking on the task of writing this book, the idea was not only to point out the errors avoid repetitive expressions, but also to give the correct usage and hints on the right use of English; certain known and unknown facts and information on this fascinating language have also been brought out. The idea is not only to make the reader learn error-free English, but also to make him learn certain finer nuances of this wonderful language. The inputs in this book have been made with the intention of making the reader a person well-versed in this language.

2

THE DEFINITION OF CORRECT ENGLISH

Recently I read an article in *The Asian Age*. The article titled "How Correct is Correct English?" talks about the yardstick of correct English. The writer says most students use a difficult complex phrase where a simple word would do the job effectively. This is because he says students tend to believe that the English language does not have room for them; that it is a secret code known only to the initiated; that the language they speak is uneducated, inferior and incorrect. Their usages reflect a corseted tone and vocabulary that strain at sophistication, and their writing lacks clarity of thoughts and expression. The writer says this is because the students are taught to worship the volcano god of correct English. Instead of being comfortable with the language, their learning makes them insecure.

Correct English is not using bombastic words or ornate phrases with which neither the user nor the listener is comfortable. Correct English is using simple, easy-to-comprehend language, and at the same time as far as possible grammatically correct English. English need not be completely 'grammar proof' to be correct; sometimes the rules can be relaxed a little to make it easy and user-friendly, and at the same time correct.

There is no such thing as correct English. That is why David Crystal, a leading scholar, titles his new history, the stories of English as *Plural*. He shows that the notion of correctness emerged only in the eighteenth century, the work of a few appointed authorities (like a few grammarians and pronunciation pundits). These people believed the language had gone out of control — too many new words, too many regional accents, too many different ways of saying things — and needed to be stabilised. Behind the linguistic anxiety lay an anxiety about status. Commercial expansion, imperial conquest and industrial revolution were creating a vast new middle class. Socially insecure "new men" began to learn from conduct manuals how to act, and dress language pundits came forward to teach them how to speak. The standard, in speech as in conduct, was politeness, defined by Samuel Johnson (himself a pundit) as "elegance of manners; gentility; good breeding". Correct English was upper class English.

Pundits made a set of rules for correct English. Polite classes were made to follow these rules. The grammarians did not hesitate to censure the likes of Milton and Shakespeare for violating rules that had not existed when they wrote. In spite of all this, most people continued to speak the stigmatised regional and class dialects (English that people spoke since the language's origin). This is not to denigrate the value of what linguists call Standard English. Standard English is defined as the language as it is used in formal contexts, the English of the press, the profession and government. It is not as narrow as correct English — it contains a surprising degree of variation — nor need it be as neurotic, since its purpose is intelligibility (rules of 'grammar police' like not ending a sentence with a preposition are irrelevant to intelligibility). Standard English is extremely useful because it allows English speakers everywhere to communicate with one another.

In this article, we get several glimpses from David Crystal's book. Standard English allows us to communicate with the past. Standardisation — given to us by the pundits — has slowed the pace of linguistic change. Standard English is the language's skeletal structure, but non-standard varieties — the language's blood, muscle and nerves — are equally valuable; they are the down-to-earth English, the language as it is lived, the vernaculars of the kitchen and the street, of youth culture and ethnic culture. They are also the enduring wellsprings of literary achievement. The genius of English is an oral one, its literature greatest when *hewing* closest to speech. One should remember that great authors are usually playwrights.

One is not averse to teaching the children to speak Standard English. But they should learn to value their own vernacular as something more than 'broken English'. To quote the example of schools in Italy, children are taught the national language without ignoring the child's native Sicilian or Neapolitan. The student who says, "The bag of books are heavy" should be corrected, but the student who says, "He be walkin' by" needs instead to learn the distinction between his first language and Standard English.

To quote another book raising similar questions, *Do You Speak American*? by Robert Macneil and William Cran, immigrants need a mastery of Standard English which becomes a ticket of cultural admission. Linguistic practice, linguistic ideology, linguistic snobbery—all these factors influence a person's English. Social

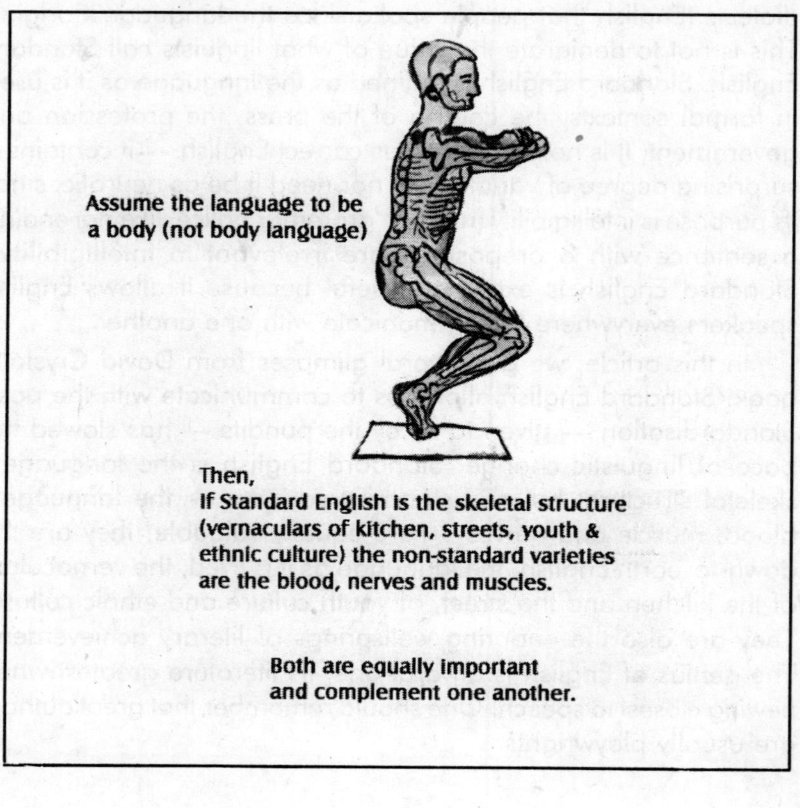

acceptance (anxious to prove they belong) is every person's dream, more so for an immigrant. So many people try to hide behind a hyper-correct lingo (lest they are rejected).

A harsh and hard English rigidly clinging to rules of grammar is to be avoided in preference to a simple and lucid English which may not be all correct from grammar's point of view.

This article raises many important issues: first it says Standard English is important; but the non-standard counterparts of English, which represents the 'down-to-earth' English, is also equally important. There are certain reasons for the students using hyper-correct lingo instead of a simple (not following the rules of grammar meticulously) lingo. Immigrants also prefer Standard English mastery as they want to use it as a passport to social acceptance. What is the definition of correct English? What are the rules for its standardisation? Are the rules (which were formulated by the self-proclaimed authorities of grammar) valid today? When we read this article, we cannot help agreeing with the argument, "How correct is correct English?" This sets one to wonder on this issue. Any sensible person should follow three basic principles while tackling such linguistic right and wrong.

Point 1 To use a simple, lucid, and as far as possible, grammatically correct English.

Point 2 To keep in mind the vernacular aspect and avoid excessive formal and ornate language.

Point 3 While using English (or any other language for that matter) one should avoid social/cultural pressures. The language must be used with freedom for effective communication and expression of thoughts.

3

CERTAIN TERMS AND THEIR MEANINGS

In many competitive exams, some terms are given and students asked to give their meaning. The answers are often wrong. In order to avoid mistakes in the interpretation of such terms, this section has been included with the students in mind.

The following section explains certain terms pertaining to English language which a person must know before he learns about various errors and how they can be corrected. Written English and spoken English are often associated with certain words. Let us try to learn in this section what they mean.

Good English is described as the English of the educated classes. Swift said 'Style' is proper words in the proper place. The concept of basic English was laid down by C.K. Ogden.

1. We often hear of the term 'RP' in reference to linguistics. RP stands for *Received Pronunciation*.
2. A *Homophone* is a word having the same pronounciation as another but a different meaning and spelling.
3. Daniel Jones devised the *cardinal vowel scale*. The number of cardinal vowels are eight.
4. *Bilabial consonants* are produced with the primary articulators (the two lips).
5. Levelling of inflexion is a characteristic feature of middle English.
6. In English the sounds |m| and |n| are *nasals*.
   the sounds |w| and |j| are *semi-vowels*.

7. An *allophone* is a variant of a phoneme.
8. A *Phoneme* is the smallest unit of a sound in a language that can distinguish two words.
9. A *Morphene* is the smallest meaningful unit in a language.
10. Articulation of speech sounds is usually described in two broad terms: place and manner of articulation.
11. The grouping of words which naturally go together through common usage is called *Collocation*.
12. Association of words is normally formed by emotional response.
13. The additional meaning that a word or phrase has beyond its central meaning is labelled as *Connotation*.
14. When a word derives its meaning from the existence of other words of a similar nature, the group of words is called its *Semantic Field*.
15. In linguistics *Dialect* means a variety of languages spoken in one part of a country.
16. An individual's language system either in speech or written form within the overall system of language is called *Idiolect*.
17. The variation of the language governed by the context or situation is called *Register*.
18. The register variation of a language determined by the subject or topic is referred to as *Field*.
19. By *Style of Discourse*, we mean the register determined by the relation between the addressed and the speaker.
20. Traditional grammar of English emphasizes the 'How and Why' of the use of language.
21. Structural grammar owes its existence to Ferdin and de Saussure.
22. Noam Chomsky wrote the synctatic structures.
23. TG grammar stands for *Transformational Generative* Grammar.

24. Grammatical arrangement of words is called *Syntax*. It is an arrangement of words in a sentence; it is the department of grammar dealing with usages of grammatical construction.
25. A *Oxymoron* is a figure of speech with pointed conjunction of seeming contradictories.
26. An *Diacritical Mark* indicates that the written letter has a particular sound.
27. A *Synecdoche* is a figure of speech in which the part represents the whole or the whole represents the part.
28. An *Anagram* is a word formed from the rearrangement of letters in another word.
29. An *Epigram* is a short witty saying.
30. A *Pun* is humorous use of a word to suggest another that sounds the same.

Did you know?

The *Talmud* and other Jewish writings use puns.

4

THE ALPHABET

The Alphabet, a book by David Sacks, has some interesting information on these fascinating entities. The following section gives a brief summary of certain interesting facts from this book.

Alphabets were a source of fancy to Ben Jonson, Samuel Johnson (who did not approve of his own initial), Descartes, Edward Lear and Kipling. Victor Hugo was not the first to be enamoured by the Latin alphabet.

A is the roof, the gable with its crossbar; or it is the greeting of two friends who embrace and shake hands—and so on, through the whole alphabet. P is the porter standing with a burden on his back. Z is lightning—it is God. In fact, A, according to this book, is a Phoenician ideogram of an ox's head, an aleph. How it became our A is described in the first chapter; Z is the subject of the last. In Phoenician it seems to have had something to do with an axe, and its principal use in English has been to differentiate between words with similar spellings and different meanings ('dose', 'doze').

The strangest thing is the way an alphabet can be taken over from an entirely alien, even unknown language—Phoenician by the Greeks, then by Etruscans "whose tongue was as different from Greek as Greek was from Phoenician". Then it was copied by the Romans whose language was as far as possible from whatever is known about Etruscan.

This book which began as a 26-part series for a newspaper is witty and cheery. The complex subject of alphabets has been dealt with expertise. The author's researches led him into archaeology, phonetics, typography, even marketing (Brand X) and throw up some odd pieces of information which, though they often belong to the Michael Caine category of facts—"Not a lot of people know that"—are interesting none the less. For Latinate Dr. Johnson the alphabet consisted of only 24 letters. He scorned J as a variant of I and V as a variant of U. He uses both in his dictionary. He has neither letter as a dictionary heading; 'jam' is followed by 'iambic'.

The minuscule 'i' received its dot only around AD 1000 because undotted, it caused confusion so that 'Y' was often used instead of i in 'hys'.

The irritating differences between English and American spellings were intentional. Noah Webster (a compiler of an American dictionary of the English language, 1828) had a political agenda. He set himself to create diversity between American and British English to assist his country's sense of identity. Some of Webster's spellings can claim to be more authentic than the British ones: *color, favor* return the words to their original Latin spellings with no intervening influence of media eval French. He tried a few oddities, 'aker' for 'acre' 'tung, for 'tongue' but these were later abandoned.

So many oddities: 'uncial' writing, an eighteenth century term referring to what became in print lower case, was so named after a remark of St. Jerome's (around AD 400) about 'litterae unciales', 'inch-high letters.'

X as a symbol of the unknown became so by typographical chance. Descartes, in 1637, in his *La Géo métrie* had equations, ABC (constants)=XYZ (variables). The typesetter ran out of Y, Z, blocks and asked if X would do. Descartes agreed "or so the story goes", David Sacks adds carefully, and there are plenty such in his book. The book becomes a bit serious at times and such tit-bits make it interesting.

As one reads this book, one gets to know a lot on various alphabets, words, their spellings. This book clears many of our doubts regarding the English alphabet and words. After learning certain facts one avoids the errors associated with the alphabet/ words concerned. Readers of this book can learn a lot on various formations of alphabets and this can aid in error-free writing and speech pertaining to the respective words and phonetic.

Interesting Facts

The author was going through certain old English journals and came across interesting facts on many letters of the alphabet (few of them have been given below).

When we learn that each letter has an interesting origin and history we become more careful in using them. A sense of responsibility arises when we start taking each letter seriously.

A Fact about letter A

This letter first appeared in ancient Phoenicia, on its side (A) and represented an OX, which was a symbol of wealth. The Greeks turned it right side up, and that is how it has been ever since!

Fact-O-File

The oldest letter of the English alphabet is O, unchanged in shape from the olden days. It was first adapted in the Phoenician alphabet (city states of Eastern Mediterranean Sea) in 1300 BC.

5

COMMON ERRORS — A CLASSIFICATION

As mentioned earlier, a person has to know the correct usage of English, and must avoid the common and uncommon errors while speaking and writing. There is a lot of difference between knowing English and knowing correct English.

In this section is a list which classifies the various common errors often committed in written and spoken English.

I. *Words*

Mistakes in words with some letters

Common spelling errors

Commonly confused words

Misused words

Using certain terms without knowing the parlance

II. *Nouns*

Errors in agreement with verbs

Errors in the use of plurals

Errors in case

III. *Pronouns*

Errors in agreement with verbs

Errors arising with the use of antecedents

Errors in case

Miscellaneous errors

IV. *Verbs*

Errors in agreement with the subject

Errors in tense

Errors in voice

Errors in splitting forms

Errors in mood

Miscellaneous errors

V. Errors arising from the confusion of adjectives and adverbs

VI. Errors in using the predicate adjective, and errors in using adverbs

VII. Errors in using modifying elements

VIII. Errors in using prepositions

IX. Errors in

a. Using conjunctions

b. Making comparisons

c. Punctuation

X. Redundancies, style, broad and vague words and miscellaneous errors in usage.

For a cup of grammatically friendly words/sentences, you need:

Half a cup — Logic and sense

2 teaspoonful of — Proper prepositions

— Suitable conjunctions

Half a cup of — Modifying elements in essential amount

— Comparisons in correct measure

Blend all ingredients well and serve on a plate of 'Style'.

Garnish generously with appropriate punctuation.

Note — This measure will serve all!

— *Literary Intelligentia and the colloquial 'abusers'.*

Every aspect of English grammar is prone to error if not used with diligence and care.

Apart from the errors in the use of nouns, pronouns, adjectives, adverbs, prepositions, conjunctions, there are other errors in English usage which include:

a. Errors in the use of singular/plural
b. Errors in the use of idioms/phrases
c. Errors in construction of sentences
d. Errors in the use of tenses, gender, articles

Errors can be committed in using words which have similar meanings; words which sound similar are also prone to errors. Modal auxiliary verbs are misused; translation and pronunciation errors also need to be considered. Proverbs are misused and misinterpreted. Errors are made while using direct/indirect speech [active/passive voice]. Punctuation errors should not be omitted while discussing errors.

Newspapers and printed materials like magazines and posters are often the common sources of errors. There can be wrong spellings, improper use of capital/small letters, wrong punctuation, inappropriate/misappropriate words and idioms, wrong abbreviations and adjectives, and distortion of sense. While considering the deliberate and not so deliberate errors, one should also consider the following:

1) Proofreading errors (errors missed while proofreading or errors introduced unknowingly during proofreading)
2) Printer's devil (errors introduced without knowledge during the printing process)
3) Misinterpretation (when the reader misinterprets something which is actually correct in all respects.)

When we consider verbs, errors can be committed with respect to tense, subject-verb agreement, tense formation. Errors can also be committed in infinitives, gerunds, and idiomatic verb expressions.

Pronoun errors can be with respect to pronoun subject-object, subject-verb agreement. Errors can occur in position of relative pronouns and impersonal pronouns.

Adjective-adverb errors include errors in comparatives, among various other mistakes.

Noun errors include errors in countable and non-countable nouns, noun-adjective usage, etc.

While discussing and classifying the errors, one should learn the basic rules/ regulations of English grammar which delineates as to what is right English and what is not so correct English. Most of the books which discuss common errors in English give pages and pages of sentences which first gives the wrong sentence, then the right sentence. The reader learns these sentences but when a new sentence is given to him to either correct it/enhance its meaning, he is unable to do so. This is because he has not learnt the basic principle but only the examples. The concept is important, not the example. If he learns the concept, he can apply it to any sentence. It is not enough if he learns that 2 plus 3 is 5, or 6 plus 2 is 8, he should know that it is addition i.e., the basic concept. This book first discusses the correct ways to pronounce, interpret, contextual use, decipher the meaning of elements of grammar (nouns, verbs, adjectives, adverbs, etc.), how to apply them in sentences and then how to avoid the common errors.

Give the hungry man a fish and you have fed him for a day; teach him to catch fish, and you have fed him for a lifetime so goes an old saying. Teaching a person the means of earning a livelihood is better than giving food for a day. This should be the aim when it comes to teaching correct English usage. Instead of pages and pages of examples (wrong and then the right usage) stress should be on principles and rules of grammar and correct usage.

What should a reader learn from such a book?

The reader should learn the application. Instead of learning the examples (wrong and right usage), he should learn the dictum of correct usage. Once he learns the basic rules for correct English, he can apply these to any given context/instant and be rest assured of an error free speech or manuscript.

6

ERRORS IN USAGE OF WORDS

Among the most common errors in usage are those which arise from confusing certain pairs or sets of words. These words are misused due to the ignorance of the precise meaning of the word. Many words have the same letters. For example, TOP and POT, CAT and ACT, GOD and DOG, TOKYO and KYOTO and so on. The slight change of a letter here and there can make a great difference to the meaning of the entire word. One has to be very careful while using such words, and must see to it that every letter of a word comes in its proper place.

Words with Same Letters

Here is a list of certain words with some letters, and one has to be very cautious that the words are spelt properly, otherwise there will be distortion of the entire sense.

1.	time	mite
2.	reap	pear
3.	rail	liar
4.	lion	loin
5.	leap	peal
6.	words	sword
7.	loop	pool
8.	teach	cheat
9.	ram	mar
10.	was	saw
11.	tool	loot

12. tour rout
13. late tale
14. mate team
15. stone tones

One should first know the correct meaning of a word before using it. One should also know the context for using a word. Each word has its unique meaning and fits only in a proper context.

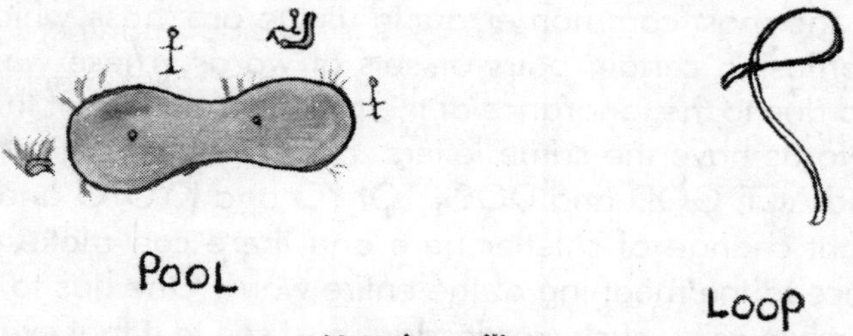

Note the spellings

Common Spelling Errors

The following words are often missplet in writing. This is because the arrangement of letters in these words are often ignored. They should be carefully studied and then should be used in writing. Let us take about five to six examples in each letter under this topic.

A

Abhorrence (means contempt)
Accent (means stress of voice)
Accident (note the double 'c')
Accommodation (note the double 'c' and 'm')
Accomplish (note the double 'c')
Aerial (note the 'e' after 'a')

B

Bachelor	(unmarried man)
Beard	(hair growth on chin)
Banquet	(feast)
Bulletin	(note the double 'l')
Blond, Blonde	(refers to hair colour)

C

Calendar	(this is index of months)
Calender	(to press in a roller machine)
Camouflage	(note the 'ou')
Cost	(refers to price)
Center	(this is American spelling)
Check	(prevent)
Cheque	(note for payment)
Cord	(rope)
Chord	(string of harp)
Cell	(cave, smallest unit of a tissue in biological parlance)
Sell	(give away at a cost)
Canteen	(note the double 'e')
Cannon	(note the double 'n')
Canon	(means a rule)

D

Diary	(daily record of events)
Dairy	(milk producing centre)
Deed	(note the double 'e')
Died	(past tense of die)
Dyed	(coloured)
Definition	(scientific description)

E

Epithet	(adjective)
Elementary	(rudimentary, simple)
Emergency	(note the 'er' and 'ge')
En masse	(means all together)
Extraordinary	(note the 'raordi'—this part of the word is important)

F

Facetious	(jocular)
Facitious	(artificial)
Fictitious	(imaginary, note the 'titi' part of the word)
Faint	(dim, weak)
Feint	(attack)
Feat	(trick or skill)
Feet	(plural of foot)
Final	(last)
Finale	(end)
Flea	(insect, note the 'ea')
Farm	(agricultural land)
Form	(printed paper)
Forum	(place for discussion)
Fort	(stronghold; note the 'rt')
Forte	(strong point; note the 'rte')

G

Goal	(destination)
Goal	(jail)
Gamble	(to play at stakes; note the 'ble')
Gambol	(play with children)

Gaze	(see)
Gauze	(thin, transparent fabric)
Glass	(transparent brittle material; note la)
Gloss	(brightness; note 'lo')
Grass	(plant; note 'ra')
Gross	(total; note 'ro')

H

Haphazard	(disorderly)
Haughty	(proud)
Hall	(big room)
Haul	(pull, drag)
Hunt	(prey; note 'un')
Haunt	(place for frequent visits; note 'aun')
Heel	(hind part of the human foot)
Heal	(cure)
Heir	(entitled to receive property)
Hair	(bristle-like growth on the head)
Hare	(an animal)
Hay	(dry grass)
Hey	(calling attention)
Hole	(hollow spot in a solid body; note 'Ho')
Whole	(entire; note 'Who')

I

Imaginal	(of an insect)
Imaginary	(fanciful)
Imaginative	(showing imagination)
Imminent	(impending)

Eminent	(famous)
Inn	(hotel; note the double 'n')
Invisible	(which cannot be seen)
Invincible	(which cannot be conquered)
Inferior	(of low quality, lower portion)
Interior	(inside)

J

Jab	(poke roughly)
Job	(work)
Jockey	(rider of horses)
Juvenile	(youthful)
Joker	(one who jokes; note the 'ker')

K

Kangaroo	(note the double 'o')
Kneel	(bend)
Knapsack	(leather bag; note the 'k' before nap)
Knot	(interwining of ropes)
Naughty	(mischievous)
Knowledge	(preception of fact or truth)

L

Laboratory	(a place where scientists carry on tests)
Lame	(crippled)
Lad	(boy)
Lade	(put cargo on boat)
Last	(end)
Lost	(missing)

List	(catalogue)
Lest	(otherwise)

M

Maid	(a woman who works as cleaner in a house)
Made	(done)
Male	(a species of men; masculine)
Mail	(post, letter)
Malign	(slander)
Message	(information)
Massage	(rubbing with oil)
Mite	(small value, a small organism)
Might	(power)
Morn	(morning)
Mourn	(cry)

N

Nation	(people of a country; note the 'Na')
Notion	(opinion; note the 'No')
Neighbour	(note the 'bou')
Notorious	(infamous)
Noted	(distinguished)

O

Odd	(strange)
Ode	(a form of poetry)
Offence	(note the double 'f')

P

Pact	(agreement)
Pail	(bucket)
Pale	(sickly)
Pain	(suffering)
Pane	(window frame)
Principle	(rule; note the 'ple')
Principal	(head; note the 'pal')

Q

Quadruped	(four-legged animal)
Quadruplet	(four children born together)
Quatrain	(a stanza of 4 lines)
Queue	(note the double 'ue')

R

Rebel	(a person who fights against conventions)
Recipient	(note the 'cipie')
Reluctant	(note the 'tant')
Requisition	(an authoritative request)
Razor	(note the 'zor')

S

Scenery	(natural features of a place)
Sole	(heel of the shoe)
Soul	(spirit)
Squander	(waste)
Scapegoat	(person bearing blame for others)

T

Theme	(subject of discussion)

Thirsty	(craving a drink)
Torture	(infliction of pain)
Traffic	(note the double 'f')
Trespass	(note the double 's')

U

Umbrella	(note the 'rella')
Utilitarianism	(materialism)
Unanimous	(with one accord)
Umbilical	(of the navel)
Utter	(speak; note the double 't')

V

Various	(different)
Vacancy	(emptiness; unoccupied place)
Vendetta	(blood feud)
Versatile	(having talent for many things)
Variety	(state of being diverse)

W

Weak	(slender)
Week	(seven days)
Weigh	(note the 'gh')
Weather	(season)
Whether	(if; it also means to bear with)
Womanise	(be promiscuous)

X

Xylophone	(note the 'Xylo'; it is a musical instrument)

Y

Yacht	(light sailing vessel; note 'cht')
Yolk	(the white of an egg)

Yoke	(harness on bulls)
Yummy	(delicious; note the double 'm')
Yell	(shout; note the double 'l')

Z

Zeal	(enthusiasm; note the 'ea')
Zest	(keen enjoyment or interest)
Zinc	(a metal; note the 'c', it is not 'k')
Zipper	(zip fastener; note the double 'p')
Zen	(form of Buddhism; it is ze and not 'se')

In the beginning of this chapter, we talked about the incorrect use of words due to confusion in certain pairs or sets of words. The following section gives some examples of this mistake.

1. Accept—Except

Accept, a verb, means 'to receive'. *Example*: I accept your gift.

Except may be either a preposition or a verb.

Example (preposition): Every girl is here except Sita.

As a verb 'except' means to 'make an exception' of.

Example (verb): We except Gopal from the responsibility.

If one realises the meaning involved, one would never have any difficulty in using the right word in the right context.

Wrong: I shall except the invitation card when he brings it.
Right: I shall accept the invitation card when he brings it.
Wrong: They excepted the report file given to them.
Right: They accepted the report file given to them.
Wrong: The doctors accepted certain possible diseases from the patient's diagnosis.
Right: The doctors excepted certain possible diseases from the patient's diagnosis.

2. All right—Alright

The term all right is correct; the word alright is non-existent in acceptable usage.

Wrong: Everything is alright in the army camp.
Right: Everything is all right in the army camp.

3. All together—Altogether

The words *all together* have the meaning of 'everyone in or at the same location'. The word *altogether* means 'entirely'.

Wrong: We were there altogether for the first birthday of Anusha.
Right: We were there all together for the first birthday of Anusha.
Wrong: They were all together unanimous in their decision.
Right: They were altogether unanimous in their decision.

4. Amount—Number

Amount & Number

This bottle has a small amount of perfume.

The number of boys playing basketball is three.

The word 'amount' is used to denote quantity. The word 'number' is used when the objects involved can be counted.

Wrong: The amount of animals in the zoo was small.
Right: The number of animals in the zoo was small.
Wrong: We had a large amount of girls participating in the beauty contest.
Right: We had a large number of girls participating in the beauty contest.
Wrong: There was a small number of honey in the jar.
Right: There was a small amount of honey in the jar.
Wrong: The number of money needed for paying the fees was high.

Right: The amount of money needed for paying the fees was high.

5. Anxious—Eager

The word *anxious* should be used only when anxiety is involved; it should not be used as a substitute for the word *eager*. The word *eager* means 'full of desire or enthusiastic'.

Wrong: I am anxious to read the new book of my favourite author.

Right: I am eager to read the new book of my favourite author.

Wrong: Sita was eager to know about her brother's condition admitted in the hospital.

Right: Sita was anxious to know about her brother's condition admitted in the hospital. (Here anxious is being used in the right context as Sita's anxiety has to be portrayed.)

Able and *capable* are two words often confused. The word *able* means having the ability to perform a given act, and *capable* means having the adequate capacity to do or to make.

'All ready' and 'already' are another set of words often misused. The words 'all ready' mean that everything is in readiness. The word 'already' on the other hand is an adverb which pronounces the idea that an action is complete at the present moment.

There is often confusion regarding the three words 'allusion' 'delusion' and 'illusion'. Using these three words correctly is simply a matter of understanding the definition of each. The word 'allusion' means a 'reference'. It is the noun form of the verb *allude*. The word 'delusion' is defined as a 'fixed aberration of the mind'. The word 'illusion' means a situation wherein a person has misinterpreted the data of his senses, i.e., he has made an 'error in vision or mental perception'. Once the clear difference between the meaning of these three words is understood, one can never make a mistake in using them in the correct contexts.

Similarly, there is a bit of confusion in using similar sounding words: Alumna and Alumnae—Alumnus and Alumni. 'Alumna' is a female graduate. Its plural is 'Alumnal'. An 'alumnus' is a male graduate. Its plural is 'alumni'.

Another set of words often posing confusion in usage is 'apt,' 'liable', 'likely'. Informal usage permits the synonymous use of these three words, but formal usage recognises a precise use for each. 'Apt' means 'has an aptitude for'; 'liable' means 'answerable to or for'. 'Likely' means 'a high degree of probability'.

Other examples of such confusing words are 'aware-conscious' 'awful-awfully'. Once the person who is using such similar words understands the exact meaning of these words, he will have no problem in choosing the right word in the right context.

Having discussed certain similar sounding confusing words under letter A, we will now discuss such words in other letter. Though there are many such words we will discuss only a few common ones. In B, we have two such common words. One is the set 'balance and remainder'. 'Balance' can be used as a synonym to remainder when discussing matters of money and in keeping of records.

Wrong: We plan to keep the rental car for the balance of the day.

Right: The right option is *remainder of the day.*

Right: Our cash records show a cash balance of Rs. 6316.25.

Right: For the remainder of his holidays, he relaxed.

Another confusing pair of words is 'between-among'. The word 'between' can be used when there are only two persons, objects or ideas under consideration. If three or more are involved, 'among' should be used. It is a better choice.

Most of the people find a little confusion in using words bring and take. 'Bring' is used in situations where something is being moved toward the speaker. The word 'take' is used when something is being moved away from the speaker.

Under the letter 'C' we have have many sets of words which pose difficulty in correct use. 'Can-may'; 'certain-sure'; 'complected-complexioned'; 'continual-continuous'. Once the person goes through the exact meaning and context of their use, he will have no errors. The word 'certain' and 'sure' are adjectives. The words 'certainly' and 'surely' are adverbs. This should be clearly understood. The word 'complexioned' is the correct form; 'complected' is accepted only as a colloquial word.

'Can not' or 'cannot'? This question is also often asked by many persons. The correct form is now almost universally considered to be the single word 'cannot'.

Wrong: I can not attend the wedding.
Right: I cannot attend the wedding.

Under the letter D, we have confusion in using two sets of words: Data-datum. The word 'data', when used synonymously with facts, is plural; when it is used synonymously with information, it is singular. The word 'datum' meaning fact in the singular form of the word 'data' (facts).

Wrong: The data (facts) is correct.
Right: The data (facts) are correct.
Wrong: The data (information) are inspiring.
Right: The data (information) is inspiring.
Wrong: The datum are subject to challenge.
Right: The datum is subject to challenge.

'Disinterested-uninterested': The term 'disinterested' means not influenced by personal or self-interest; the word 'uninterested' means 'not interested'.

Under the letters E and F, we have many words which are confused. 'Each other-one another' is one set like the previously discussed 'between and among'.' Each other' is used when two persons are involved, and the expression 'one another' is used when three or more persons are involved. 'Enthuse and enthusiastic': the word 'enthusiastic' is the accepted form of usage.' 'Enthuse' is best avoided.

Wrong: This plan does not make me enthused.
Right: This plan does not make me enthusiastic.

'Farther-Further': The intechange of these two words is not a serious error, but there is a distinction between their uses. 'Farther' is used in speaking of physical distance, i.e., situations in which distances can be measured. 'Further' is used in matters wherein physical measurement is not possible.

'Fewer-less': 'Fewer' is used when an actual count can be made; the word 'less' is to be used when referring to quantity.

Right: Sita made fewer mistakes with the new calculator.
Right: We have less trouble with that old machine now.
Wrong: We have less teachers than the previous year.
Right: We have fewer teachers than the previous year.
Right: We have fewer students in our class than we had last year.

'Former-latter': When one uses these words only two persons or objects must be under consideration. If more than two are involved, these words must be avoided.

Coming to next letters I, L, M there are many words that confuse the speakers and writers. 'Imply-infer' in i; 'lay-lie', 'learn-teach', 'lend and loan', 'loose and lose' in L.

The words 'imply' and 'infer' have some distinction; 'imply' should be used by speakers and writers. 'Infer' should be used by listeners and readers.

'Lay-lie': The verb 'lay' is transitive (i.e., takes an object) while the verb 'lie' is intransitive (does not take an object). The principal parts of 'lay' are *lay* (present), *laid* (past), *laid* (past participle) and *laying* (present participle); while the principal parts of 'lie' are *lie* (present), *lay* (past), *lain* (past participle), and *lying* (present participle).

'Learn-teach': When one is the receiver of facts or any other type of lesson he is learning. When he is imparting the information to a second person he is teaching.

Wrong: We shall have to learn that child to be obedient.
Right: We shall have to teach that child to be obedient.

'Lend and loan':'Lend' is to be used as a verb and 'loan' as a noun.

Example: I shall lend Ramu Rs. 300
I shall make her a loan of Rs. 1,000.

'Loose and lose':The word 'loose' means free, the opposite of tight.

Example: The shirt I bought for Gopal was too loose for him.

'Lose' means to suffer a loss.

Example: I do not want to lose my Rank in the class.

Hema does not want to lose her position in the class.

Ramu's mother warned him not to lose his purse in the crowd.

Under the letter 'M' we have many words posing confusion in usage. 'Majority-plurality' are two such words. The term 'majority' means at least one more than half. The word 'plurality' means the highest number within a great number.

'May-might': The word 'may' is often confused with the word 'can'. It is also confused with the word 'might'. The word 'may' has the meaning of 'future possibility'.

Example: The hot weather may remain for a month.

The word 'might' on the other hand has the meaning of a future condition that is dependent upon a hypothesis.

Example: If she would help, I might also participate.

'Memoranda-memorandum': 'Memoranda' is the plural form of the word 'memorandum'. 'Memorandums' is also acceptable as a synonym for 'memoranda'.

'Moral-morale': 'Moral' as a noun means 'a lesson'.

Example: This story has a moral.

As an adjective, 'moral' means good or characterised by that which is right.

Example: Our teacher is a moral man.

'Morale' means mental condition, general spirit, frame of mind.

Example: Her morales are questionable.

Let us now discuss some words in letters P and R.

'Party-person': The word 'party' is permissible as a substitute for the word 'person' only in legal usage. In other kind of writing, one must be careful not to interchange these words.

'Practicable-practical': The word 'practicable' means 'that which appears to be capable of being put into the practice'. *Example*:Gita said her plan was practicable.

The word 'practical' means that something is known to be workable or effective.

Example: We were given a practical suggestion for evaluation.

'Precede-proceed': The confusion between the use of these two words can be avoided by understanding the correct meaning of the two words. The word precede means 'to go before'.

Example: The student leader will precede the students in the march post.

The word 'proceed' means to 'move forward'.

Example: The boss asked his subordinate to proceed with the proposal.

'Principal and principle': The word 'principal' used as a noun means the 'head of a school, a main participant, a sum of money invested'. As an adjective 'principal' means 'main or most important'. The word 'principle' is a noun. It means 'a rule, a law, an idea that is part of a code of behaviour'.

'Prophecy and prophesy': The word 'prophecy' is a noun. The word 'prophesy' is a verb.

Example: My prophesy is that he will win the game.

I prophecy that she will win the match.

'Proved-proven': The word 'proved' is always either a verb or part of a verb phrase.

Example: The student proved the theorem.

The word 'proven' must always be used as an adjective.

Example: This herb is a proven remedy for cough.

'Provided-providing': 'Provided' is the past participle of the verb *provide*. It is also a conjunction meaning 'if'. 'Providing' is the present participle of the verb *provide*. A common error arises with the use of 'providing' for 'provided' as a conjunction.

'Raise-rear-rise': The word 'raise' should not be used when referring to the upbringing of one's family. However, 'raise' is used when speaking of other forms of life like plants, animals. 'Rear' means breed and look after (animals) and also bring up (children).

Example: The kennel owner specialises in raising poodles.

We reared our children in Illinois.

The word 'raise' is a transitive verb (takes an object) while the verb 'rise' is an intransitive verb (does not take an object).

The principal parts of raise and rise are

Raise	Rise
Raise (Present)	Rise (Present)
Raised (Past)	Rose (Past)
Raised (Past participle)	Risen (Past participle)
Raising (Present participle)	Rising (Present participle)

The use of the verb 'arise' follows the same pattern as the verb 'rise'.

In the final section of our discussion on commonly confused words, let us see some words in letters S and W: 'shall and will'. The distinction between the use of 'shall' and 'will' is now restricted to formal usage. 'Shall' is used with the first person and 'will' with the second and third persons.

'Should-would': This follows the basic pattern of usage as 'shall and will'.

'Sick-disgusted': The word 'sick' should not be used as a synonym for displeased or bored. 'Disgusted' means revulsion, loathsome, etc.

'Set-sit': The verb'set' is transitive. The verb 'sit' is intransitive.

'Suspect-suspicion': The word 'suspicion' is a noun. The word 'suspect' is a verb. 'Suspicion' cannot be used in the place for 'suspect'.

Right: I suspect his motive.
Right: I suspect her intention.
Right: My suspicion is that he is the culprit.

'Way-ways': The word 'way' is singular. The word 'ways' is plural. One must avoid using the plural form for the singular.

Right: Sita's house is a long way from the bus stop.
Right: There are three ways to travel from the park to the station.

We have discussed common spelling errors, words with the same letters which need to be spelt properly and also the commonly confused words.

In this next section, we will be seeing some commonly misused words. In everyday written and spoken English certain words are commonly misused. For example, the word 'average'. It is 'standard regarded as usual'. It also has meanings like commonplace, everyday, mediocre, medium, middling, moderate, normal, ordinary, run of the mill, standard, typical, unexceptional, usual. Because of so many meanings, this word is often misused. Strictly speaking, this word should be used only in situations wherein an arithmetical computation can be made.

Words like 'alibi', 'alternative', are often misused. 'Alibi' means 'proof that one was elsewhere'. It also means 'excuse'. Precise usage demands that it be used only in legal terms. The word 'alternative' has the meaning 'usable instead of an other'. It can also be used as 'any of two or more possibilities'. But this word should be used only when 'two choices' are involved. In strict sense, 'alternative' means the second of two choices.

When we consider letter 'C', 'client, climax' are two words often misused. 'Client' means a person using the services of a professional person. The word 'clientele' means clients. This word 'client' is often misused as a 'customer'. But it should be restricted to legal parlance. A person presenting with a case to a lawyer, he becomes the client of that lawyer. The word 'client' is also by insurance agents who enrol prospective 'clients' for their various policies. Here the word 'client' refers to the buyer of insurance policies. The word 'climax' means a point of greatest intensity or interest. But this word is used to denote acme, culmination, height, high point, peak, summit, zenith. Preuse usage demands that the word 'climax' be used in its literary sense—the point in a story where the action is resolved into a single, inescapable conclusion.

Let us take the letter 'D'.'Dilemma': This word is often misused. This word means a situation in which a difficult choice must be made. But it is often used in situations like 'difficult situation', catch 22, fix, impasse. Strictly speaking, it must be used wherein one faces just 'two choices, either of which is unsatisfactory or otherwise objectionable'.

Similarly, the word 'delusion' means a false belief or impression, but this word is misused in various situations to denote error, illusion, misapprehension, mistake, misconception.

In the letter E we can see many words being misused: essential, extra, enable, ego, entice. The word 'enable' means 'to give ability, to make able'. It can also be used 'to give the authority or means to do something'. But this word is being used in many contexts—'allow; authorize, empower, entitle, license, permit, qualify'. There is nothing wrong in using this word in such contexts, but it should be used only when 'ability is given'.

'Essential' means 'absolutely necessary', 'fundamental', but this word finds use to say crucial, indispensable, key, vital, necessary, requisite, basic, inherent, innate, intrinsic, quintessential. 'Essential' is an absolute adjective. Therefore, one object can never be 'more essential' than another. Hence, this word has to be used with caution.

'Extra' as an adjective which means additional; more than usual or expected. As an adverb, it means 'more than usually' or 'in addition'. As a noun, it means 'extra thing, person employed as one of a crowd in a film'. As an adjective, it is used to specify added, additional, auxiliary, further, spare, supplementary. In addition to all the above , the word 'extra' is used as a prefix to denote outside, beyond (extracellular, extraordinary).

A common error arises with the attempt to make the word 'extra', an adverb meaning unusually or very.

'The new chocolate tasted extra good' is a wrong sentence. 'The new chocolate tasted very good' is the correct statement.

The word 'ego' is often misused. It means self or self-esteem (as a noun). There are so many words arising from it like egocentric (adjective) means self-centred; egoism, egoist, egoistic, egotism,etc. Care must be taken while using this word. 'Ego' should be strictly used to say about self-esteem. Anger, rage, etc., should not be confused with ego.

'Entice' means to attract by offering something pleasant. Allure, attract, coax, inveigle, lure, tempt,wheedle, all these are often denoted by the word 'entice'. Care must be taken to restrict the use of the word 'attract'.

When we consider the letter F words like fix, farce, fulsome are all often misused. The word farce means light comedy. It also means absurd and useless proceedings, pretence. It is to be used with caution keeping both the meanings in mind.

The word fix has several meanings like, put something firmly in place; establish, specify; repair; direct steadily, but the colloquial use of the word 'fix' to mean 'arrange fraudulently' has often resulted in the misuse of this word. As a noun,'fix' means 'an awkward situation'. It also means a position determined by taking bearings. 'Fix up' means organise, provide.

As a verb, the word is used to say attach, anchor, fasten, make fast, secure, stick, pin. It also means agree on, arrange, conclude, decide, set. When used to mean 'repair' 'fix,' it is used to mean mend, cure, correct, patch up, rectify. As a noun, 'fix' is used to mean catch-22, difficulty, etc.

In the precise sense, the word means to 'make fast'.

Example: The wooden sheet was fixed to the wall.

While using the word in the colloquial sense, one should be careful as it can mean a predicament or to arrange fraudulently.

The word 'fulsome' means excessive and it also means insincere. This word should not be associated with the word 'full'.

Considering the letters I, L, M, we can say the words impeach, invaluable, livid, mutual are all often misused.

'Impeach' means accuse one of a serious crime against the state and bring one for trial. This word became very familiar word during the 'Monika Lewinsky Bill Clinton' scandal in USA. Clinton was supposed to face an impeachment motion and there was even a fear that he may be removed from the president's office. This word means to bring a man to trial with the object of removing him from office if found guilty. It does not mean 'to remove from the office.'

The word 'invaluable' means 'having value too great to be measured'. It is an absolute adjective. It cannot be therefore qualified by a modifier.

The word, 'livid' means a bluish-grey colour; colloquially it means furiously angry. Care must be taken while using this word. 'Livid' is an absolute and consequently one object cannot be more livid than another. It should not be used to mean other colours.

The word 'mutual' means 'felt or done by each to the other'. This word conveys the idea of something reciprocal or interchangeable. Colloquially it is often used to mean something common to two or more. It is thus used to denote reciprocal, reciprocated, common, communal, joint, shared. The correct use of this word is restricted to denote reciprocal. It should not be used to mean something common.

Coming to other letter words like orphan, per, plus, sadistic, unique, vital all are misused. The word 'orphan' means a child whose parents are dead but in true sense only one parent need be deceased in order to term a child an orphan. The words 'per' and 'plus' are often misused. The word 'per' is a reposition meaning for each, in accordance with, by means of. 'Per annum' for each year, 'per capita' for each person, 'per cent' in or for every hundred. This word 'per' should not be used as a synonym for 'in keeping with' or 'in accordance with', in the strict sense. It is to be used only in standard business transactions. The word 'plus' means with the addition of; above zero. As an adjective, it means more than zero, more than the amount indicated. As a noun, it means 'advantage'. In formal English, the word 'plus' should not be employed as a synonym for the conjunction 'and'.

The word 'sadistic' means sexual pleasure from inflicting or watching cruelty. It should not be used to mean strong interest in gory details or simply cruelty.

The word 'unique' means being the only one of its kind, unequalled. It is often used to denote something incomparable, inimitable, matchless, peerless, unequalled, unparalleled. This word 'unique' should not be used to mean odd, strange. The word 'unique' cannot be modified.

As an adjective, vital means essential to life, essential to a thing, existence or success. 'Vital statistics' means those relating to population figures. Colloquially, it means measurement of a woman's bust, waist, hips. The word 'vital' is used to denote critical, crucial, essential, fundamental, imperative, indispensable, key, necessary. This word also denotes alive, animated, lively, energetic, spirited, vibrant, vivacious. 'Vital signs' refers to pulse (heart rate), respiration rate, etc., in medical parlance. The word 'vital' should be used only to denote 'that which is necessary for existence'. It should not be used to convey the idea of that which is merely important or highly desirable. It should be used when 'life' is involved. This justifies the term 'vital signs' which means pulse, breathing rate, papillary reflex which are parameters of utmost importance in an emergency or a critical state of a patient to detect his condition, whether severe or dangerous.

We must also learn some terms which are often misused. 'De facto' means in fact. 'De jure' means by law. 'Joie de vivere' means feeling of being healthy, enjoyment of life. 'Seldafe dendo' means in self-defence. 'Totidem verbis' means in so many words. We often see these words being misused in wrong contexts. A person must first get the right meaning of the word, know the parlance—legal, medical, literary, context to use the word before using the word. Formal and colloquial English have their own rules and one should not violate these rules. Cautious, careful use of words in speech and written English comes from practice. Practice alone can make one avoid errors and speak/write perfect English.

Our discussion on errors pertaining to words will not be complete without mentioning similar-sounding words which can lead to errors while being used. Knowing the correct meaning will solve this problem.

A

adapt and adapt
advice; advise
affect; effect
allude; elude
appraise; apprise

B

beside; besides

C

capital; capitol

carat; carrot

cite; sight; site

compile; comply

D

detracted; distracted

devolve; evolve

E

elegant; eloquent

eminent; immanent; immanent

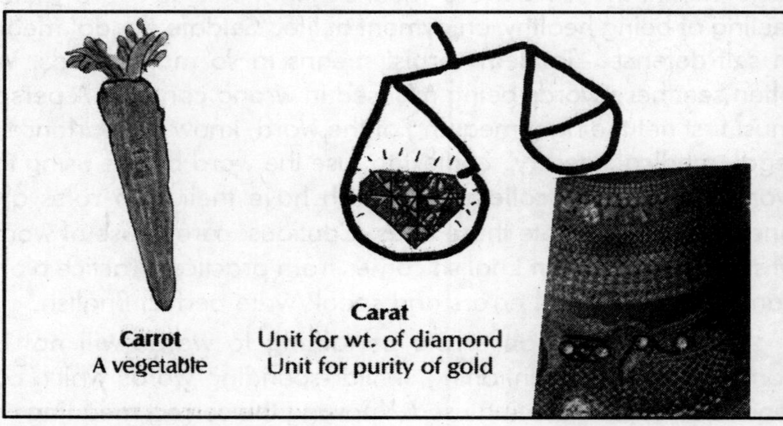

Carrot
A vegetable

Carat
Unit for wt. of diamond
Unit for purity of gold

F

foreword; forward

G

gorilla; guerilla

H

human; humane

horde; hoard

I

in; inn

incite; insight

ingenious; ingenuous

irrelevant; irreverent

L

loath; loathe

P

perpetuate, perpetrate

persecute, prosecute

personal; personnel

perspective; prospective

precede; proceed

profuse; profess

R

relay, relate

repel, repeal

S

staple; stable

stationary; stationery

supplement; supplant

T

their; there, they're

troop, troupe

W

weigh, way, whey

weather, whether.

7

SEPARABLE PAIRS

The following list presents a group of paired words that could be difficult to differentiate in meaning. But once the meanings and pronunciation are learnt, the chances of error are very less.

1. **Eject**
To throw out
To expel
To force out
Example: To eject a heckler

Inject
To put or force into
to inject a vaccine
Example: To inject a vacine.

2. **Introspection**
Self-examination
The act of looking within
Example: To be given to retrospection.

Retrospection
A survey of past events
Looking back on old days oneself.
Example: To indulge in introspection.

3. **Induce**
To persuade
To lead or move to action
Example: To induce a person to leave.

Deduce
To infer; to derive as a conclusuion
Example: to deduce a suspect, guilt from the evidence.

4. **Induct**
To install, as in an office
Example: To induct the new vicar.

Deduct
To subtract to take away
Example: To deduct an item from taxable income.

5. Affluent	**Effluent**
A rich person; Having an abundance of goods.	Stream that flows from a larger stream or body of water
Example: An affluent population.	*Example*: River Jordan is an effluent of sea of Galilee.
6. Reputed	**Imputed**
Considered or regarded	Ascribed or attributed (to); charged (usually referring to a fault or misdeed)
Example: Reputed to be wealthy.	*Example*: The crime was imputed to him.
7. Euphony	**Cacophony**
Pleasing or harmonious sounds	Harsh or discordant sounds
Example: The euphony of his phrases.	*Example*: The cacophony of an orchestra tuning up.
8. Erupt	**Disrupt**
To burst or break forth, as a volcano	To break up; to rend as under; to split
Example: The geyser erupted.	*Example*: To disrupt a meeting.
9. Digress	**Regress**
To stray from the main theme of a discourse	To go back; to move backward; to degenerate
Example: to digress for a moment.	*Example*: some plant species tend to regress.
10. Denote	**Connote**
To be the sign of; to indicate	To suggest; to signify; to imply
Example: Clock hands denote the hour.	*Example:* Exceptional intelligence in a child usually ionnotes intelligence ancestors.

After going through the above words, the reader would have learnt the following points:

1. Though several words sound similar, they have wide difference in their meanings; like affluent, effluent.
2. Several of the above words are opposites:
   Eject-Inject
   Euphony-Cacophony
3. Some words are similar in meaning but are not synonyms. They have some difference in their meanings:
   Erupt-to burst/break forth
   Disrupt-to break up
4. Certain words have something in common:
   Introspection
   Retrospection
5. Both talk of some kind of examination:
   One is 'self 'examination'.
   The other is a survey of past events.
6. Also the pronunciation of words are important when using them
   a f' lü ent-ef' lü ent.
   u' fo nëkā kōf' onë.

Errors in pronunciation are very common in these words and one must avoid it at any cost for effective, clear verbal communication.

Errors in Words Ending with 'able'

Given below are 24 words ending in 'able'. But 11 of them should end in 'ible'. The reader can check the ones that he believes should be spelt 'ible'. Answers are given below in this page:

1. imperceptable
2. convertable
3. unpredictable
4. dependable
5. contemptable
6. laudable
7. irrepressable
8. definable
9. flexable
10. divisable
11. reputable
12. digestable
13. detestable
14. suggestable
15. inconceivable
16. delectable
17. reproducable
18. inconsolable
19. pervertable
20. inscrutable
21. compatable
22. deplorable
23. attachable
24. transmittable

(Wilfred Funk)

The reader will be quite perplexed after going through the list given above. It is often seen that errors in 'able' and 'ible' are committed and the person is not even aware of his mistake.

Answers

imperceptible
convertible
contemptible
irrepressible
flexible
divisible
digestible
suggestible
reproducible
pervertible
compatible

8

WORDS BEGINNING WITH 'IM'

There are many words beginning with 'im'. It is often seen that many persons make mistakes in the meanings of these words. The following section presents certain words beginning with letters 'im' and their correct meaning. This section will be useful for many persons who had doubts on such words and who misused them.

1. **Imputation**—Act of charging; attribution, especially of fault or crime.
2. **Imbroglio**—Complicated situation; serious misunderstanding.
3. **Imbue**—To saturate; to cause to become impressed or penetrated as, to imbue with wisdom.
4. **Impost**—Tax or levy; especially a customs duty.
5. **Impoverish**—To make poor; to exhaust the strength or richness of.
6. **Imminent**—About to happen (usually of danger).
7. **Importunate**—Insistent; urgent in demanding; annoying in pertinacity.
8. **Impermeable**—Not permitting to passage, especially of fluids, impervious.
9. **Impassive**—Without emotion; apathetic; showing no feeling.
10. **Impasse**—Predicament affording no escape; deadlock.
11. **Impeach**—To accuse; to charge with crime or misdemeanour; especially to charge a public official with misbehaviour in office. Also, to call into question.

12. **Import**—Meaning or significance, as of a word, phrase or document.
13. **Impale**—To transfix upon a pointed object; to torture or punish by fixing on a sharp stake.
14. **Impede**—To hinder; to limit or obstruct.

IMPEDE
means to hinder

15. **Impious**—Irreverent; lacking in respect; wicked.
16. **Imposture**—Fraud or trickery to gain an end; deception under a false or assumed character.
17. **Impalpable**—That cannot be felt; intangible; so fine and delicate as not to be easily discerned.
18. **Impetuous**—Hasty, impulsive, rash.
19. **Impromptu**—Improvised; made done or utters on the spur of the moment
20. **Improvident**—Thriftless; lacking foresight or forethought failing to provide for the future.

Malapropism

In Sheridan's play 'The Rivals', Mrs. Malaprop continually used long words in the wrong places. The following section gives a list of paired words which may prove troublesome. If one wants to avoid the reputation of being called a 'Malaprop', he must learn the meanings of these words and use them correctly.

1. **Complement:** Number or quantity required to fill or

complete. *The vessel carried its peacetime complement of the men.*

Compliment: Expression of praise or admiration. *He paid her a compliment for her art deco.*

2. **Resource:** Reserve source of supply, strength or support. *To exhaust every resource.*

   Recourse: Application for or resort to help. *To have recourse to a library.*

3. **Tortuous:** Full of twists or bends. *A tortuous mountain trail.*

   Torturous: Cruelly painful; agonising. *Hours of torturous worry.*

4. **Conscript:** Recruit; one compulsorily enrolled in one of the services. *Conscripted into the army.*

   Transcript: Handwritten or typed copy of an original; *A transcript of the trial.*

5. **Disquisition:** Formal discourse based on careful research; elaborate essay.

   Inquisition: Through investigation; judicial or official inquiry, often with the intent to fix guilt.

6. **Disport:** To amuse or divert, to disport oneself in the water.

   Deport: To banish; to exile; to transport. *To deport a criminal alien.*

7. **Colloquy:** Conference; mutual (and usually formal) discussion. *Colloquy about literary affairs.*

   Obloquy: Abusive language; public defamation calumny. *To subject a person to obloquy.*

8. **Temporise:** To pursue a policy, a delay; to avoid immediate decision in order to gain time. *He didn't dare refuse, so he tried to temporise.*

   Extemporise: To make or do on the spur of the moment, without preparation; to improvise. *To extemporise a speech.*

9. **Hypercritical:** Excessively fault finding; unfairly critical. *Hypercritical review.*

   Hypocritical: Pertaining to one who professes to be what he is not in order to win approval. *A hypocritical person.*

10. **Prescribe:** To order or direct; to dictate; to lay down as a rule of action. *To prescribe the hours of study.*

    Proscribe: To prohibit; to denounce; to condemn. *To proscribe smoking.*

9

THREE-LETTER WORDS

We all understand words of three letters, but can we always explain them? It is often found that people get mixed up with these words and their meanings. The result is misuse of the words.

1. Nib—Point, as of a pen.
2. Van—Forefront; position of leadership. *To be in he van of the reform movement*. Short for 'vanguard'.
3. Yaw—To move unsteadily or off course, as a ship in storm. *To yaw in heavy seas.*

To move unsteadily on or off course.

4. Wan—Pale, pallid; of a sickly hue, weak.
5. Wry—Twisted. *A wry smile* (a grimace that indicates displeasure or disgust).
6. Eke—To supplement. *To eke out one's income.*
7. Con—To study; to read with care. *To con a lesson.*
8. Nub—The gist, or point. *The nub of a story.*
9. Oaf—Blockhead or dunce, simpleton.

10. Vie—To strive for superiority; to put forth great effort to out do others; to compete. *To vie for once's attention.*
11. Fen—Marsh or swamp.
12. Don—To put on, as a garment. *To don a coat.*
13. Dun—To press for payment. *To dun a debtor.*
14. Rue—To regret bitterly; to have cause to be sorry for. *To rue one's action.*
15. Ebb—To decline; to wane; to subside; to recede. *My interest began to ebb.*
16. Era—A period in time. *The Christian era.*
17. Ply—To urge persistently; to keep furnishing or supplying; shortened form of 'apply'. *To ply a guest with question.*
18. Par—Equality; footing or basis of similarity. *To be on par with one's colleagues.*
19. Wag—A droll, humorous fellow; perhaps shortened from wag halter; rogue; joker; one likely to swing from the gallows.
20. Ado—Unnecessary activity; bustle; fuss. *Much ado about nothing.*

Though these words look all too familiar and easy, they are often misused and their meaning misinterpreted. This is only the tip of an iceberg. There are so many of such three-letter words that are misused. Proper study of their meaning is important before they are used.

Different Meaning, Same Spelling!

There are many words which have the same spelling but different meanings. These words can be easily misinterpreted if a person does not know the context in which they are being used, and also the two different meanings of similar spelt words. Given below are such words.

1. Dispense—To dole out in portions; to distribute. *To dispense rations.*

   Dispense—To for go; to give up or relinquish. *To dispense with a summer holiday.*

2. Contend—To assert or maintain; to argue. *To contend that one's opponent is wrong.*

   Contend—To compete; to vie; to strive in competition or rivalry. *To contend for a prize.*

3. Submit—To yield or defer to authority. *To submit to security regulations.*

   Submit—To offer or present as one's opinion. *To submit that the charge is not proven.*

4. Access—Admittance or passage. *Access to the records.*

   Access—Outburst, fit of passion. *Access of fury.*

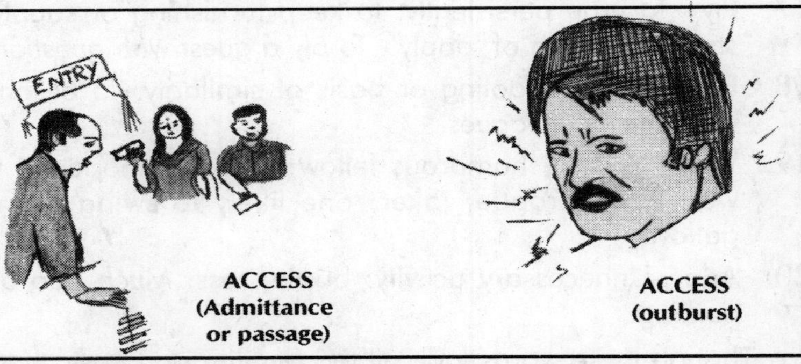

ACCESS (Admittance or passage) **ACCESS (outburst)**

5. Assume—To take for granted; to suppose. *To assume the truth of a statement.*

   Assume—To adopt; to take on or up. *To assume a haughty mien.*

6. Retainer—Fee paid (often in advance) to secure prior claim to professional services. *A retainer agreement.*

   Retainer—one who is attached to and serves a person or household. *A family retainer.*

7. Prone—Inclined; disposed. *Prone to criticise.*

   Prone—Prostrate; flat, especially face downward. *To lie prone on the floor.*

8. Regard—To look at; to watch. *To regard the speaker closely.*

   Regard—To heed; to show respect for. *To regard one's wishes.*

9. Expedition—Journey for a specific purpose. *An expedition of discovery to the* Arctic.

   Expedition—Speed; dispatch. *The work progresses with expedition.*

10. Maintain—To keep in condition; to take care of; to sustain; to uphold. *To maintain one's reputation.*

    Maintain—To affirm; to assert. *To maintain that the plan want work.*

11. Consequence—Result or effort of a preceding action. *Consequence of war.*

    Consequence—Importance. *A matter of consequence.*

12. Arrest—To stop, to check or hinder. *To arrest progress.*

    Arrest—To seize on and fix. *To arrest the attention of the audience.*

13. Qualify—To modify; to limit; to soften. *To qualify a statement.*

    Qualify—To meet the requirements; to be or become qualified or fit. *To qualify for office.*

14. Resolve—To make clear; to explain; to dispel or remove. *To resolve all doubts.*

    Resolve—To determine, to decide. *To resolve to act.*

15. Sheer—Downright; utter; unmitigated. *Sheer nonsense.*

    Sheer—Steep, perpendicular. *A sheer cliff.*

16. Assurance—Boldness, confidence. *To have complete assurance.*

    Assurance—Guarantee, pledge. *To receive an assurance of support.*

17. Reflect—To ponder; to think carefully. *To reflect on the speaker's words.*

    Reflect—To bring or cast discredit on. *To reflect on a person's reputation.*

18. Concur—To agree. *All the judges concur in the opinion.*

Concur—To coincide, to get together. *International traffic laws do not always concur.*

19. Remit—To send money as in payment for goods.

    Remit—To refrain from enforcing. *To remit a penalty.*

20. Compromise—To adjust or make a settlement by concessions. *To compromise a dispute.*

    Compromise—To expose to suspicion or disrepute. *To compromise a prospective witness.*

10

WORDS OF FRENCH ORIGIN

The English language contains many adopted French words which have sustained their French pronunciation. Given below are 20 such words with there correct pronunciation and meaning.

1. Cliché (klë shã)—Trite phrase; hackneyed or stereotyped expressions. *A cliché about the weather.*
2. Finesse (finess')—Artfulness, delicate skill; cunning. *He handled the difficult situation with great finesse.* Literally 'fine'.

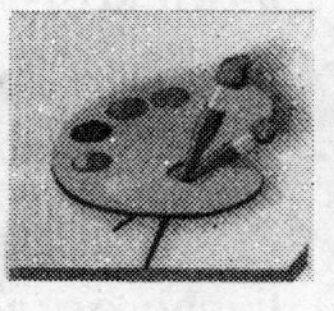

FINESEE (artfulness) The Pronouciation is (fin ess)

3. Pique (Pèk)—Feeling of resentment, especially from wounded pride. *Harsh words said in a fit of pique.*
4. Cuisine (Kwìzèn')—Style of cooking. *Italian cuisine.*
5. Carte Blanche (Cart blahnsh')—Unrestricted authority. *To give an emissary Carte Blanche* (literally 'white card'; an authorisation signed in blank allowing recipient the right to fill in any conditions he pleases).
6. Naïve (nah ëv')—Unsophisticated, ingenuous; artless. *A naïve person.*
7. Rendezvous (Rahn' day voo)—Meeting by appointment at a fixed place or time. *To arrange a rendezvous.*

8. Ennui (ôn' wè)—Boredom; feeling of weariness and dissatisfaction. *To suffer from ennui.*
9. Nuance (nü ahns')—Shade of difference; delicate gradation. *Subtle nuances of colour.*
10. Distingue (dîs tang' gay)—Distinguished, as in manner of superior bearing. *One who looks distingue.*
11. En Rapport (ahn ra pawr')—Literally in harmonious agreement; in sympathetic relation. *To be enrapport with one's neighbour.*
12. Amour (ah moor')—Love affair; intrigue. *To have an amour.*
13. Faux pas (fo pah)—Breach of good manners or conduct. *A shocking faux pas.*
14. Dossier (dos i a)—Collection of papers or memoranda documents relating to a particular subject. *Dossier on a legal case.*
15. Vis-à-vis (vè zah ve')—In relation to. *Salary vis-a-vis the national average.*
16. Piquant (pè kant)—Interesting and stimulating; charmingly lively; agreeably challenging. *A piquant sauce.*
17. Entente (ahn tahnt')—Understanding, especially between governments. *The entente cordiale between Britain and France.*
18. Pot Pourri (Po Poore')—Medley; mixture. *Pot pourri of old music hall sketches.*
19. Savoir-Faire (sã vwahr' farè)—Literally 'to know how to act'. Hence readiness in proper and gracious actions. *A diplomat famous for his savoir-faire.*
20. Entrée' (ahn' trã)—Right to enter. *Entrée into inner circles.*

Proper Words in Proper Places

The more words you have at your command, the better you are equipped to express yourself effectively. This must be one's principle in learning to write and speak error-free English. The following section gives 20 keywords and their meanings. Pronunciation of certain words are also given to prevent wrong pronunciation.

1. Spurious (spü rì us)—Not genuine; counterfeit. *A spurious painting*.
2. Fulsome—Excessive; cloying; disgustingly overdone. *Tulsome praise*.
3. Conclave—A secret council or meeting. *A political conclave*.
4. Languish—To lose strength and animation; to grow weak. *To languish in prison*.
5. Captious (kap' shus)—Unreasonably fault finding; hypercritical. *Captious critic*.
6. Conciliatory—Soothing, tending to reconcile; mollifying. *A conciliatory manner*.
7. Amalgam (amal' gam)—A combination or mixture. *An amalgam of racial strains*.

LANGUISH
(to become weak)
ex: to languish in prison.

8. Congenial (kon jen' yal)—A kindred in spirit. *A congenial companion*.
9. Sinecure (si ni kur)—A profitable job requiring little work.
10. Crass—Crude; gross; stupid. *A crass inquiry*.
11. Inundation—A flood; overspreading of any kind. *Inundation of sightseers*.
12. Scurry—To hurry; to hasten; to scamper. *To scurry along* (perhaps a blend of scatter and hurry).
13. Potentate—A person having great power. *Feted like a potentate*.
14. Riposte (ri post')—Sharp, quick reply. *A clever riposte*.
15. Abysmal (a biz' mal)—Bottomless. *Abysmal ignorance*.
16. Colossus—An object (or person) of great size. *An industrial colossus*.

17. Addiction—A slavish habit. *Addiction to alcohol*.
18. Anomalous (a nom' alus)—Deviating from the common rule abnormal. *An anòmalous situation*.
19. Parody—To imitate for comic effect or in ridicule. *To parody a song*.
20. Cajole—To wheedle; to coax or persuade with flattery or other enticement. *To cajole a child into eating*.

11

DOUBLE-TAKE WORDS

Double-take words can lead us astray because of their close resemblance in meaning or spelling.

1. **Punctual**
   On time; prompt.

   Punctilious
   Attentive to details of conduct duties. *A punctual start.*

   Both these words have a common origin from the Latin Punctus (Point).

2. **Imperial**
   Pertaining to an empire or having supreme authority. *Nation with imperial ambitions.*

   Empirical
   Based or acting on observation or experiment rather than theory. *A sailor's empirical knowledge of navigation.*

3. **Opposite**
   Situated on the other side facing, front to front or back to back; completely different. *On the opposite side.*

   Apposite
   Appropriate for the purpose; well expressed. *An apposite comment.*

4. **Sanguine**
   Habitually hopeful, confident.
   Even when ill he has a sanguine attitude.

   Sanguinary
   Bloodthirsty; accompanied by or delighting in bloodshed. *The enemy's sanguinary atrocities.*

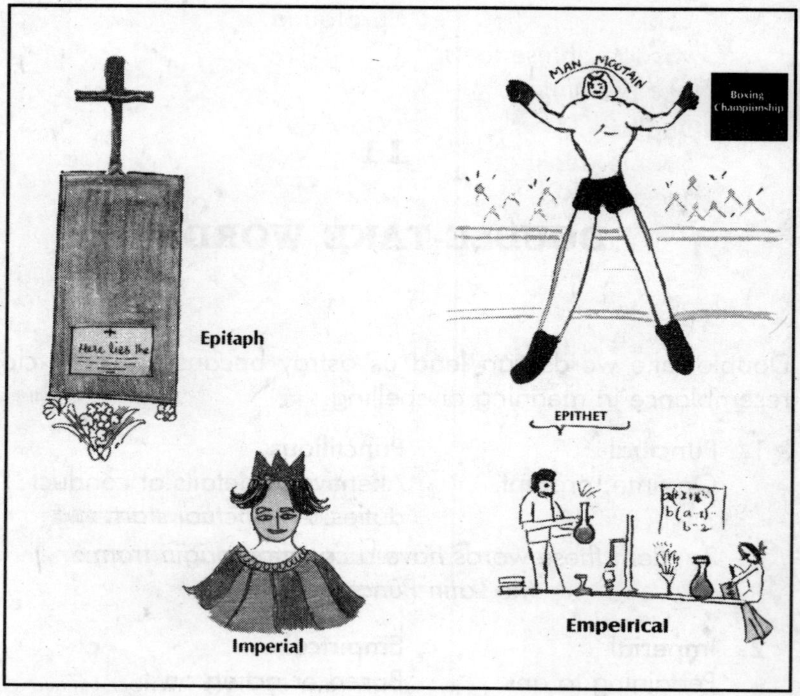

5. **Epitaph**
Inscription on a tomb or monument in memory of the dead.

Epithet
Word expressing quality or attribute; title. *The Epithet "man mountain" was applied to a wrestler.*

6. **Bathos**
Anticlimax; descent from the sublime to the commonplace. *The bathos of saying a doctor needs ethics, skills and a stethoscope.*

Pathos
Quality that excites pity or sadness. *The pathos in the movie touched the hearts of million.*

7. **Obtuse**
Slow of perception;

Abstruse
Hard to understand;

	stupid, dull. *He was too obtuse to take the hint.*	profound.
8.	**Duplicity** Double dealing; deceitfulness. *The spy's carefully concealed duplicity.*	**Duplication** Replica; exact copy; the art of duplicating. *To avoid duplication of effort.*
9.	**Hypocritical** Insincere; false.	**Hypercritical** Excessively or severely critical.
10.	**Sanctimonious** Making a show of sanctity or piety.	**Pious** Devout; religious.

Wasn't the journey through these double-take words interesting? Readers must be careful in using these words. Any hurry in using these words without proper thinking can lead to glaring errors.

Foreign Words

English has borrowed freely from other languages. We have already discussed certain words of French origin. In this section we will be seeing words adopted from other languages; their meanings; pronunciation and how to use them without any errors.

1. Pogrom (Po' grúm)—Organised massacre of helpless people; mass slaughter of human beings. *To launch a pogrom.* This is a Russian word (means devastation).
2. Aficionado (a fí see õ nah' doh)—Ardent fan; enthusiastic follower, devotee. *An aficionado of cricket.* This word is from Spanish, aficionar meaning to inspire affection.
3. Safari (sã fah' ree)—Hunting, exploring or sightseeing expedition. *To join a wildlife safari to African game parks.* This word is Swahili, from the Arabic *Safara* (travel).
4. Tycoon (tye koon')—Business magnate; influential leader. *A wealthy industrial tycoon.* From Japanese *Taikun* (great prince).

5. Kudos (kew' doss)—Praise for achievement; acclaim; honour; glory. *Kudos to the winning team*. From Greek *Kydos*.

(Business Magnate)

6. Bonanza (Bō nan' za)—Windfall; rich strike in gold or silver mining; something that yields a large profit sudden wealth. *Bonanza in oil*. From Spanish (fair weather, prosperity).
7. Kiosk (kee' osk)—Small open booth; outdoor news-stand, bandstand or telephone booth. From Turkish – *kiúshk* (pavilion), Persian – *kúshk* (palace).
8. Vendetta (ven det' a)—Blood feud between clans or families with continuing retaliatory acts of vengeance long after an offence. From Italian (vengeance).
9. Siesta (see es' ta)—Afternoon nap or rest customary in hot countries; any short sleep. *To take 15 minute siesta*. From Latin *Sexta hora* (noon) literally the sixth hour after sunrise.
10. Sarong (sã rong')—Loose skirt of coloured cloth worn by Malaysian men and women. From Malay (sheath).
11. Wanderlust (wan' der lust)—Strong desire or irresistible longing to wander or travel. From Middle high German, from *wandern* (to wander) and lust (desire).

12

PLAIN AND FANCY WORDS

There are certain words which are plain and there are some which are fanciful. English language has both plain and fancy words in plenty. Errors can be committed in the use of both these kind of words. This section gives a list of 20 words, plain and fancy, alternating with each other. These words are often misused, mispronounced and misinterpreted in meaning. Read on for the correct meaning and context of use.

1. Scrimp—To be extremely frugal; save painstakingly; be stingy. *Scrimp and save to pay the bills.*
2. Table d' hôte (tah bluh dote)—This is a very fancy word not much known or used. This word can be used in the wrong context as it is less familiar. The word means a meal in a restaurant offered at a fixed price. *The table d'hote menu offers good value.*
3. Sheath—Protective, close fitting case for a knife blade or some other object. *The sheath round a cable.*
4. Equipoise (Ek wì poise)—Equilibrium; equal weight or balance. *The equipoise of international peace was shattered by war.*
5. Tangible (Tan jì b'l)—Real and definite; able to be touched; easily understood. *A tangible reward of money.*
6. Cachet (Cash ay)—Prestige; a status symbol. *The cachet of certain cars.*
7. Gawky—Awkward; clumsy; ungainly; from gawk, to stare stupidly. *A shy, gawky teenager.*

8. Sangfroid (sahng frwah)—This is again a fancy word, meaning cool; self-possession or composure in difficult circumstances. *To face an ordeal with sangfroid.*
9. Jetty—Structure projecting out over a body of water to protect a harbour or make a landing pier.
10. Recherché (ruh share shay)—Extremely rare; carefully sought out. *A concert of recherché baroque music. A recherche' restaurant.*
11. Pert—This is a plain word meaning lively; also, saucy or impudent. *A pert child.*
12. Mandarin (Man der in)—Influential person; member of an elite group. *A literary mandarin.*
13. Peal—The loud ringing of bells; any sustained sound, as of thunder or laughter. *The joyful peal of church bells.*
14. Double entendre (doo blahn than dr')—Word or phrase suggesting two meanings one of which is usually indelicate.
15. Jaunt—Outing; excursion; short pleasure trip. *He made weekend jaunts to the seashore.*
16. Bona fide (bona uh fide ee)—commonly used fancy word, meaning in good faith; with sincerity. *A bona fide offer also authentic or genuine.*
17. Hoax—Trick or deception, especially a practical joke. *A hoax phone call.*
18. Cire cumlocution (sir kum loh kew shun)—Wordiness; evasive or indirect way of saying something. *The fondness of academics for circumlocution.*

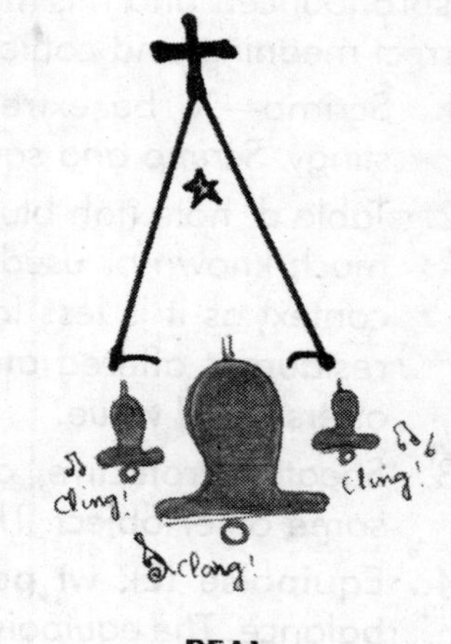

PEAL
The joyful peal of church bells.

19. Grit—Pluck; courage; determination and endurance. *Needing a lot of grit.*
20. Contretemps (kawn truh tahn)—A very fancy word; means embarrassing mishap or social blunder.

You should use a word—plain or fancy—only when you are confident of its meaning and context of usage. Just to sound good you should not use a fancy word. A simple plain word which effectively conveys the meaning is as good as its fancy substitute. If a person wants to write a very *ornate essay* and he knows some fancy words, their meaning and the context to use them, he can do it. Caution is to be followed while using words as they can change the meaning of a sentence if misused.

Valuable Words

Over two hundred years ago, the following 20 words appeared in a document that altered history: America's declaration of independence. Today their meanings are virtually unchanged. It is important that a person must known to use these words without any mistakes. Read these words and their meanings. Understanding the context of their use will help one in avoiding errors. Note their pronunciations.

1. Dissolve (dì zolv')—To end. *When... it becomes necessary for one people to dissolve the political bands...*
2. Endow (en dow')—To provide with a talent or quality; to give property. *Endowed by their creator with uncertain unalienable rights.*
3. Obstruct—To block; impede. *He has obstructed the administration of justice.*

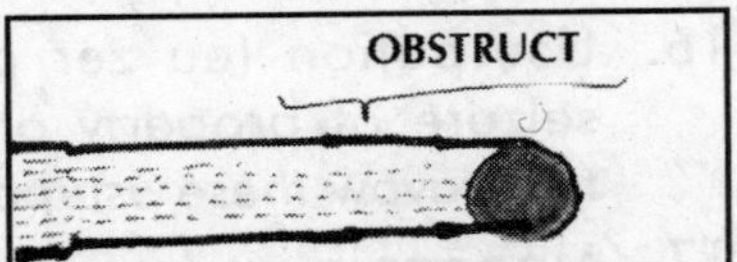

To Block / Impede. here, fow of a liquid.

4. Prudence (proo' dens)—Sound judgement, careful foresight. *Prudence... will dictate that governments.*
5. Disposed (dis pòzd)—Inclined towards. *Mankind is more disposed to suffer....*

6. Invariably (in varc abl)—Constant; not changing/ varying. *Pursuing invariably the same object.*
7. Multitude (mul' tu tewd)—A great many; large number of persons or things. *He has erected a multitude of new offices.*
8. Constrain (kon strane')—To compel; bring about by force. *The necessity which constrains them to alter their former systems of government.*
9. Tyranny (tir' a nee)—Oppressive government; dictatorship. *The establishment of an absolute tyranny over these states.*
10. Candid—Impartial; fair. *Let facts be submitted to a candid world.*
11. Arbitrary (ar bi trer ee)—Based on one's own nations; not guided by law or rules. *Establishing there in an arbitrary government.*
12. Relinquish (rì ling' kwish)—To give up; surrender; abandon. *Relinquish the right of representation.*
13. Inestimable (in es' tì ma b'l)—Beyond calculation, invaluable; too great to be measured. *A right inestimable to them.*
14. Compliance (kom ply' ans)—Yielding to a demand; conforming. *Fatiguing them in to compliance with his measures.*
15. Endeavour (en dev' or)—To attempt earnestly; work hord or dutifully with a definite purpose. *He has endeavoured to prevent.*
16. Usurpation (eu zer pay' shun)—Unlawful or unjust seizure of property or power. *We have conjured them to disavow these usurpations.*
17. Magnanimity (mag na nim tee)—Nobility of spirit; generosity. *We have appealed to their native justice and magnanimity.*

18. Rectitude (rek tì tewd)—Honesty; uprightness; adhering to rules of right and justice. *Appealing to the supreme judge of the world for the rectitude of our intentions.*
19. Insurrection (in ser rek′ shun)—Revolt; an uprising but not yet a full rebellion. *He has excited domestic insurrections amongst us.*
20. Redress (rè dres′)—Reparation of wrong; amends, as for a loss. *We have petitioned for redress in the most humble terms.*

Readers who have gone through the above 20 words would be surprised to see that words which appeared 200 years back in American declaration of independence have the same meanings even today. The meanings should be well assimilated and must be used in the right contexts?

13

NEW WORDS

In the last section we read about 200-years-old words. Thousands of new words have entered. The following section deals with 20 words and their meanings and pronounciations.

1. Digital (Dij it' l)—Based on numerals or digits. *A digital watch showing the time in numerals*. First recorded use of this word is 1938.
2. Quisling (kwiz ling)—Traitor. *We have a quisling in our midst*. This word was first used in 1940.
3. Cannibalise (kany bal ize)—To take spare parts from one thing for use in others. *To cannibalise one aircraft to keep others flying*. First used in 1943.
4. Vegan (Vee g'n)—First recorded use of this word is in 1944. This word means a strict vegetarian eating no animal flesh or product; contraction of veg (etari) an.
5. Redeploy (ree d' ploy)—To send to a new place or task. *To redeploy troops*. This word was first used in 1945.
6. Ergonomics (er go Nomix)—This word first came into use in 1950. The study of efficiency at work is called ergonomics. *To apply the laws of ergonomics to manning levels*.
7. Brinkmanship (Brink m'n ship)—Art of advancing to the brink of war but not engaging in it. *The brinkmanship of US threats to use nuclear weapons in the urban crisis*. First recorded use of this word is 1956.

8. Psychedelic (sy kuh del ik)—Awareness altering, usually of drugs that generate hallucinations or distorted perceptions. *Vivid psychedelic art*, said to depict drug induced visions. First recorded use of this word is in 1957.

'Psychedelic'

9. Ombudsman (om budz m'n)—Complaints investigator. *The ombudsman who inquires into citizen allegations of National Health Service malpractices*. First recorded use of this word is in 1959.
10. Circadian (ser kay dee un)—This word was used in 1959 for the first time. This word means occurring about once daily. *The desire to sleep at night is part of our circadian rhythm*.
11. Numerate (new muh rut)—This word came into use sometime in 1959. The word means able to use numbers, familiar with basic principal of mathematics and science. *Applicants for banking jobs are expected to be numerate*.
12. Pseud (sude)—Pretentious person. *Pseuds and intellectual craze-mongers*. This word came into use only in 1962.
13. Byte (Bite)—Group of digits (in computer language). *Computer information is arranged in Bytes*. First recorded use of this word is in 1964.
14. Street wise—It is a colloquial American word; this word has been in use from 1965. It means knowledgeable about the

hazards of city life. *Street wise youths with the cunning to side step trouble.*

15. Tachograph (tak oh grahf)—First recorded use of this word is 1968. It means travel time recorder. *Tachographs in lorries show whether drivers exceed permitted speed or hours at the wheel.*
16. Reggae (reg ay)—Type of West Indian music with a strong off-beat. *Bob Marley was a leading exponent of reggal*. This word came into use in 1969.
17. Shambolic (sham bol ik)—First recorded use of this word is in 1970. It means chaotic. *She left her room in a shambolic state*.
18. Flexitime (flex y time)—Variable working hours. *Workers on flexitime choose arrival and departure times within an agreed total of average daily or weekly hours*. The word came into use only in 1972.
19. View data (vew day tâ)—Televised text. *The prestel system, providing subscribers with view data information on screen*. The word came into use in 1975.
20. Yomp—This word is one of the very recent words that came into use in 1982. It means to march over difficult terrain carrying heavy equipment. *The Royal marines yomped across the bleak Falklands countryside.*

Since these are new words many persons make mistake in their use and pronunciation.

Pronunciation—Very Important in Speech

It is not just what you say, but the way you say it that gets results. This section has a list of 20 words which are often mispronounced. Some are hard going, others have multiple pronunciations. Some of the words given below are also misinterpreted in regard to their meaning. This section gives the correct pronunciation and the meaning.

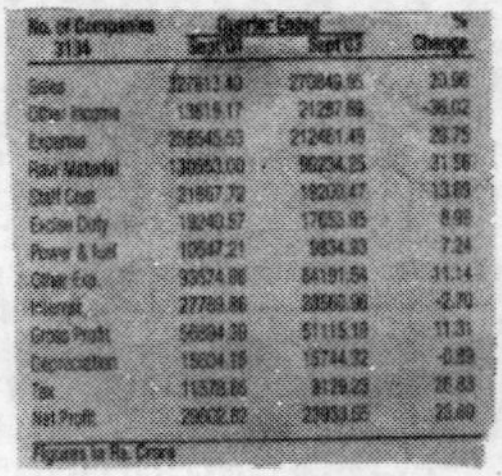

No. of Companies 3134	Quarter Ended Sept'08	Sept'07	% Change
Sales	227613.43	270849.95	23.96
Other income	13619.17	21287.86	-36.02
Expense	258545.53	212461.49	28.75
Raw Material	138653.00	98234.25	31.56
Staff Cost	21667.72	19200.47	13.89
Excise Duty	19240.57	17653.95	8.98
Power & fuel	10547.21	9834.33	7.24
Other Exp.	93574.86	84191.54	11.14
Interest	27769.86	28560.96	-2.70
Gross Profit	56894.39	51115.18	11.31
Depreciation	15034.15	15744.32	-0.89
Tax	11578.86	9179.23	25.83
Net Profit	29602.82	23933.55	23.69

Figures in Rs. Crore

Pronounciations

DATE uh

DAT uh

DATA

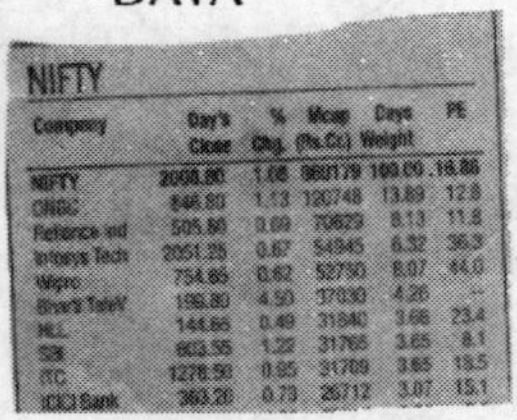

NIFTY

Company	Day's Close	% Chg.	Mcap (Rs.Cr.)	Days Weight	PE
NIFTY	2068.80	1.08	960179	100.00	18.86
ONGC	846.80	1.13	120748	13.89	12.8
Reliance Ind	505.80	0.09	70623	8.13	11.8
Infosys Tech	2051.25	0.67	54945	6.32	36.3
Wipro	754.85	0.62	52750	8.07	44.0
Bharti Tele	199.80	4.50	37030	4.26	--
HLL	144.65	0.49	31840	3.66	23.4
SBI	603.55	1.22	31765	3.65	8.1
ITC	1276.50	0.85	31709	3.65	13.5
ICICI Bank	363.20	0.73	26712	3.07	15.1

1. Data (date uh; dat uh)—This word means information; facts to be used as basis for a decision, or for a computer to process.
2. Ragout (rã goo)—Highly seasoned meat and vegetable stew.
3. Clique (kleek; click)—Small exclusive group that suggests snobbery.
4. Respite (res pit; res pyte)—Spell of relief, rest or delay, usually from a distressing situation.
5. Facade (fuh sahd)—False or superficial appearance.
6. Pot Pourri (pott poo ree; pott poori)—Scented mixture of dried flowers and spices; any collection of unrelated items; musical medley.
7. Harass (har us; huh rass)—To trouble, worry; vex by repeated attacks.
8. Archetype (ahr kih type)—Original model; in psychology the universal, subconscious images of certain recurring symbols. (This word is often mispronounced.)
9. hors d'oeuvre (or duvr)—Appetiser usually served before a main course.
10. Cacophony (kuh kof uh nee)—Harsh and conflicting sounds; dissonance.
11. Era (ear uh)—Period of history that is noted for some important event or distinctive characteristics.

12. Otiose (oh shee ose; oht ee ose)—Useless; serving no real purpose and therefore ineffective.
13. Coup (koo)—Master stroke; sudden brilliant and successful action.
14. Schism (siz'm; skiz'm)—Separation into opposing groups.
15. Flaccid (flak sid; flas id)—Flabby; lacking firmness; limp.
16. Polygamy (puh Lig uh mee)—A plural marriage in which a man or woman has more than one spouse at a time.
17. ignominy (ig noh min ee; ig noh inee)—Disgrace, public dishonour.
18. Cachet (kash ay)—Prestige; distinguishing mark or feature.
19. Chimera (kih mir uh; kye heer uh)—Wild fancy; absurd creation of the imagination. In Greek mythology a monster with a lion's head, a goat's body and a serpent's tail.
20. Trait (tray; trayt)—Distinguishing feature in character, appearance, or habit.

14

WORD PAIRS

The word pairs given below, although similar in sound and spelling, differ in meaning. These words are often misused in context and meaning. Read these words, their meanings, pronunciation and use them in the right context.

1.	**Climatic (klye mat ik)** Concerning weather or climate. *Desert climatic conditions.*	**Climactic (klye mak' tik)** Relating to climax. *Constituting the highest* point or culmination. *The climactic moment of his life.*
2.	**Abjure (ab joor')** To renounce, forswear put aside. *To abjure a claim.*	**Adjure (a joor')** To command or charge solemnly direct; earnestly entreat. *To adjure a witness to speak the truth.*
3.	**Inculcate (in' kul kate)** To instil; implant; impress upon the mind by repetition. *To inculcate a sense of responsibility in the young.*	**Inculpate (in' kul pate)** To implicate; incriminate. *To inculpate bystanders in the rioting..*
4.	**Monetary (mon'itree; mon'i tree)** Financial; pecuniary relating to carriage or currency. *Gold based monetary system.*	**Monitory (mon'i toree)** warning; admonishing. *A monitory proverb.*
5.	**Elusive (ee loo' siv)** Evasive; hard to grasp;	**Illusive (I loo siv)** Deceptive and misleading

tending to slip away or escape. *An elusive solution to the problem.*

only apparent; unreal. *Illusive hopes for peace.*

6. **Immure (i mure')**
To wall in; shut up; imprison. *To immure the trouble makers.*

Inure (in ure')
To accustom (one) to accept something undesirable; habituate. *To inure troops to hardship.*

7. **Appraise (a praze')**
To evaluate; determine the worth or merit of; set a price on. *To appraise a diamond.*

Apprise (a priz)
To inform; give notice to; tell. *To apprise the accused of his rights.*

8. **Insidious (in sid' i us)**
Treacherous; having a gradual and cumulative effect; subtle. *An insidious person*

Invidious (in vid' i us)
Repugnant; injurious; creating ill will; resentment or envy. *Invidious remarks.*

9. **Ascent (a sent')**
Upward slope activity; advance in status or reputation. *A meteoric ascent to fame.*

Assent (a sent')
Consent; acquiescence. *To give assent to a proposal.*

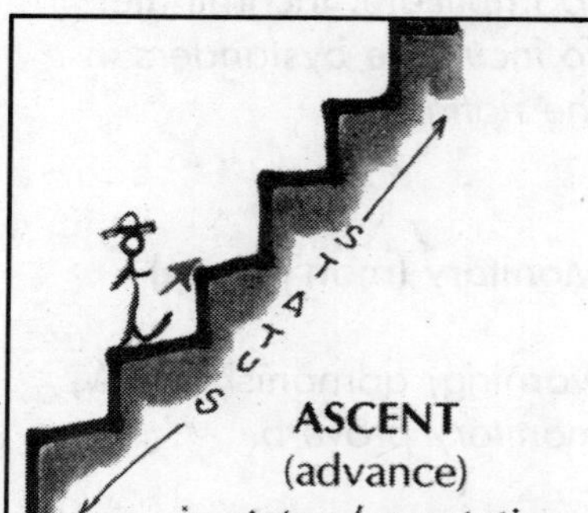

ASCENT
(advance)
in status / reputation

ASSENT
(consent green signal to a proposal)

10. Disburse (dis burs')	**Disperse (dis pers')**
To pay out; expend.	To scatter, break up and move in different directions.
To disburse campaign funds in strategic electoral districts	*To disperse a crowd.*

The above section shows a fascinating list of similar sounding and spelt words. Their meanings are of course very different. One cannot substitute these words one for another. Word pairs like *ascent-assent; monetary-monitory* and *appraise-apprise* are the most confused pairs. One needs to learn the spelling correctly before embarking on using them. While using them in speech, pronunciation must be perfect, otherwise it can sound wrong. Words like ascent and ascent have similar pronunciation and one must try to express the right word by emphasising the context in which the word is used. Practice of both spelling and pronunciation can completely avoid the error in their usage.

Errors in Latin Phrases

In this section are 20 Latin phrases that are still in everyday use. They are often mispronounced, misused in context and misinterpreted in their meaning and pronunciation.

1. Ad hoc—For a particular purpose. *An ad hoc committee was appointed.* Literally, 'to this'.
2. Protem—For the time being. *An executive appointed protem to a post that suddenly falls vacant* (Abbreviation of pro tempore, for the time).
3. In vitro (in vee troh)—In a test tube. *A 'test-tube baby is conceived when an ovum is fertilized in vitro.* Literally 'in a glass'.
4. Et al—'And others' is the right meaning of this phrase. *A jointly written report signed by John Smith et al.* Abbreviation of *et alii* (and others).
5. Caveat emptor (kav ee at emp tor)—Let the buyer beware. *Before a transaction where it is up to the buyer alone to ensure the purchase is good value, a lawyer may advise caveat emptor.*

6. Ad nauseam (ad naw zee am)—To a sickening extent. *The Jury heard gruesome evidence ad nauseam.* Literally means "to sickness".
7. In camera —It means 'in private'. *A meeting or trial closed to the press and public is held in camera.* Literally "in a vault".
8. Per se (per say)—In itself. *It is said to be the love of money that is the root of all evil, not money per se.*
9. Quid pro quo—Something given in return, compensation. *Concessions made as a quid pro quo for union cooperation.*
10. Ipso facto—Thereby; by the very fact that. *A minor is ipso facto ineligible to vote.*
11. Subjudice (sub joo dis ee)—not yet decided under law; *Press comment on cases subjudice is forbidden as it may influence the outcome of the trial.* Literally, 'under a judge'.
12. Ex officio (ex o fish ee oh)—By virtue of office. *Number 10 Downing Street is the ex officio home of the Prime Minister of Britain.*
13. In loco parentis (in loh koh par ent iss)—In place of a parent. *A child's legal guardian acts in loco parentis.*
14. Vox Populi (vox pop ew lee)—Public opinion. *Recent polls suggest that vox populi is for the reinstatement of capital punishment.* Literally, voice of the people.
15. Magnum opus (mag num op us)—Great, or greatest achievement of a creative career. *War and peace was Tolstoy's magnum opus.*
16. Per pro – By proxy. *A letter signed by an assistant per pro (or pp) Mr. John.* Abbreviation of per procurationem (by proxy).

17. In flagrante delicto (in flag ran ti del Ik toh) – In the act of committing an offence. *Trespassers discovered inflagrante delicto.*
18. Vade mecum (va dee may cum) – Handbook or other much used item constantly carried on the person. *A phrase book may be a tourist's vade mecum on holiday abroad.*
19. Sine qua non (sin eh kwa non) – Essential requirement. *Hospital training is a sine qua non for every doctor.*
20. In extremis (in ex tree miss)—At the point of death. *Last rites administered to a patient in extremis.*

15

LONG AND SHORT WORDS

Errors can be committed in both long and short words. No word is immune to mistakes until and unless the reader knows the pronunciation, meaning and the right context to use a word. This section deals with 10 short words (only one syllable) and 10 long words. Learn the spelling, meaning, pronunciation and the context of these words.

Short Words

1. Bray—Loud, harsh cry as from a donkey.
2. Jib—Projecting from a crane, also triangular sail on a boat. (17th century English word often mistaken.)
3. nee (nay)—Born; referring to the maiden name of a married woman. *Mrs. Mary Lincoln nee Odd.*
4. Snide (often misused word)—Insinuating, sneering. *The snide comment hurt her.*
5. Lee—The side away from the wind. *They crouched in the lee of a rock during a squall.*
6. Orb—Globe or sphere; *The bright orb of the street lamp.* This word is also used in poetic description of the eye (Latin-*orbis*).
7. Moot—Debatable; undecided. *I was a*

moot point; should they holiday in France or Italy?

8. Wry—Pertaining to anything twisted or distorted, especially a facial expression indicating displeasure, disgust. *A wry smile* also mocking *a wry humour*.
9. Puck—Rubber disc used in ice Hockey.
10. Splotch—Smear, stain or spot. *Ugly splotch on the rug.*

WRY
(a wry smile)

Long Words

1. Ambulatory—Mobile; also pertaining to walking. *An ambulatory word.* (This word is used a lot in the medical field).
2. Deferential—Respectful; yielding to someone else's wishes or judgement. *The student's deferential attitude towards his teacher.*
3. Manifestation—Evidence or indication of the nature of a person or thing. *The mechanic's repair was a manifestation of his skill.*
4. Heterogeneous (het ur uh jee nee us)—Varied; consisting of unlike people or things. *Most political parties are composed of heterogeneous personalities.*
5. Cartographer (car tog ruh fer)—Someone who makes maps.
6. Intransigent (in tran si jent)—Uncompromising; stubbornly refusing to give up an outlook or position. *The committee's intransigent policy created problems.*
7. Extemporaneous—(ek stem puh ray nee us)—unrehearsed; off hand. *An extemporaneous speech.*

CARTO GRAPHER

8. Misapprehension—Misunderstanding; mistaken idea. *A misapprehension in negotiations between workers and management.*
9. Disingenuous—Insincere; deceitful; not straightforward. *A disingenuous witness.*
10. Blasphemous—Blas fe mus; Profane, showing disrespect for God or anything held sacred or in high esteem.

Similar looking and Sounding words

Certain words not only sound similar they also look similar. When a person is reading a script he will commit mistaken if he doesn't do a careful study. The following section has a list of 10 sets of such similar looking and sounding words. Utmost caution is to be taken while using these words.

1.	**Flounder**	**Founder**
	To struggle in an awkward faltering way as if in deep snow; to make fumbling efforts. *He floundered through his speech.*	To sink; also to collapse or fail. *The project foundered.*
2.	**Notable (Note a b'l)**	**Notorious (noh tore ee us)**
	Worthy of notice for any reason; remarkable. *Notable achievement.*	Having a bad reputation; widely known in an unfavourable sense. *Charles Sobraj ia a notorious criminal.*
3.	**Exalt**	**Exult**
	To praise highly; also to raise in status or rank.	To rejoice greatly.
4.	**Allusion**	**Illusion**
	Indirect reference or casual mention of	A misconception; as, the illusion of being something

something. *An allusion to the secret formula.*

we are not; also deceptive impression. *A mirage is an illusion.*

5. **Rebuff**
To snub; give a rude refusal to someone's request.

Refute
To prove a theory wrong conclusively.

6. **Immunity (í mew nitee)**
Protection from a disease; also freedom from ordinary obligations or misfortunes.

Impunity (im pew nit ee)
Exemption from undesirable consequences.

7. **Diagnosis (dy ag noh sis)**
Identification of an illness or problem by analysing symptoms.

Prognosis (prog noh sis)
Forecast or prediction especially as to the outcome of a disease.

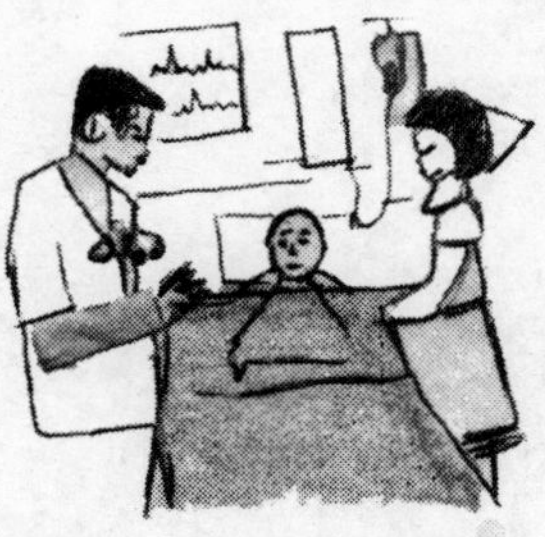

Doctor: 'I want to do a Blood Test to rule out Malaria.' He has fever and chills.
This is Diagnosis

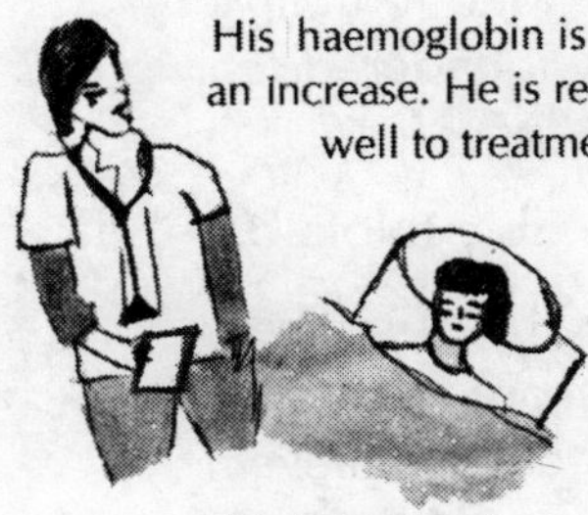

This is Prognosis

8. **Adverse (add verse)**
Whatever opposes is harmful or interferes.
Adverse winds.
Adverse effects of a drug.
Adverse circumstances.

Averse (ã verse)
Unwilling; reluctant.
Averse to getting up early.

9.	**Reconcile (rek un sile)** To bring into harmony; restore a friendship. *Reconcile their differences.*	**Conciliate (kon sill ee ayt)** To win over; overcome unfriendliness. *To conciliate an enemy*
10.	**Sententious (Sen ten shus)** Pompous, dull, moralising using famous saying to appeal. *Sententious speaker.*	**Tendentious (ten den shus)** Biased; promoting a particular cause. *A tendentious article pretending to be objective.*

16

HOMOPHONES

Homophones are words with the same sound as another but with different spellings and meanings. The words in this section are perfect homophones in the sense *they sound almost similar*. Their meanings are of course different.

1. **Phase** — A stage of development or change; a particular aspect. *This is a difficult phase in her life.*

   Faze — To disconcert, perturb. *Nothing seems to faze him*

2. **Oral** — Spoken; by, of, or, in the mouth. *An oral report.*

   Aural — pertaining to or received by the ear. *The constant loud noise produced aural damage.*

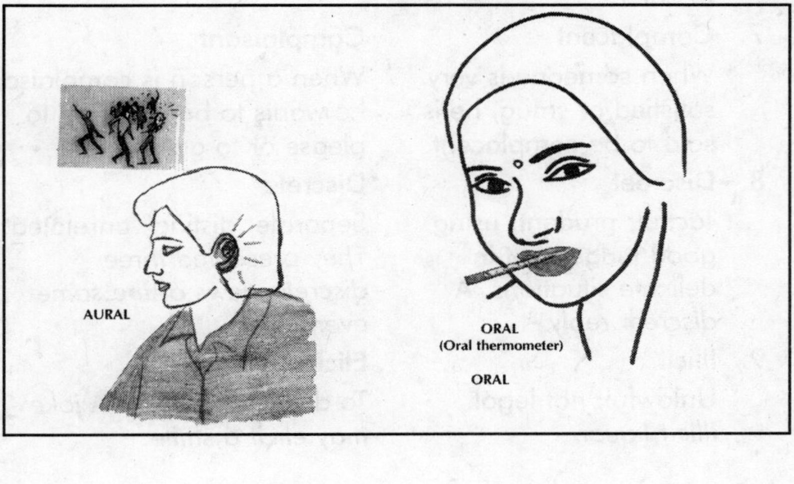

3.	**Censor** Official empowered to examine all written and spoken material and to suppress whatever is considered unacceptable. *Censor board for feature films.*	**Censer** A container for burning incense.
4.	**Elusive** Tending to slip away or escape; difficult to understand or perceive. *An elusive thought.*	**Illusive** Not real; based on a false or misleading idea; deceptive. *Illusive dreams of instant wealth.*
5.	**Principle** Fundamental truth or belief; primary element. *It is not the money, it is the principle.*	**Principal** Chief, first in rank or importance. *Principal conductor of the orchestra.*
6.	**Cue** Hint; guiding suggestion; an actor's signal. *The music was the actor's cue to enter.*	**Queue** A line of people awaiting their turn. *A queue at the ticket booking counter.*
7.	**Complacent** When someone is very satisfied or smug, he is said to be complacent.	**Complaisant** When a person is complaisant he wants to be obliging, to please or to go along.
8.	**Discreet** Tactful; prudent; using good judgement in delicate situations. *A discreet reply.*	**Discrete** Separate, distinct, unrelated. *They presented three discrete views of the same event.*
9.	**Illicit** Unlawful; not legal. *Illicit liquor.*	**Elicit** To draw out; evoke. *A joke may elicit a smile.*

10. **Horde**
Crowd, gang; troop of tartar or other nomads. *Hordes of people flocked out of the refugee camps.*

Hoard
Stock; store (especially of money). *The old miser counted his hoard of gold coins every night.*

One more set of words which needs mention here is 'quite' and 'quiet'. 'Quite' is an adverb meaning 'completely'; 'quiet' is an adjective meaning with little or no sound, silent. These two words are often misspelt and produce confusion. The letter Q has another set of homophones – quiver and quiver. Quiver (noun) is a case for holding arrows; quiver (verb) – shake or vibrate with a slight rapid motion. One has to be very careful in using these homophones. There should be clarity and precision in using them in speech and in manuscripts. First learn them and then use them. This must be the rule to avoid errors in their usage.

Errors in words and Prefix 'Pro'

'Pro' is a hard working prefix that means 'before', 'forward' or 'forth'. In this section we will be discussing some words all with the prefix 'pro'. This section gives the right meaning, right pronunciation and right use of these words.

1. Proverb—Short familiar saying. *'Practice makes perfect' is a proverb.*
2. Procrastinate—To delay, put off.
3. Prohibit—To forbid; outlaw.
4. Proficient (pro fish ent)—Skilled, competent.
5. Profane—To treat with disrespect anything revered or honoured.
6. Protrude—To stick out; project.
7. Profuse—Lavish; overflowing; excessive. *Profuse compliments.*
8. Proprietary (pro pry uh ter ee)—privately owned.

PROTRUDE
See the usage: Hari's Belly seems to protrude out!

9. Prospectus—Description of a business venture, investment opportunity. *A stock prospectus.*
10. Promulgate (prom ul gate)—To announce officially; proclaim. *To promulgate the law.*
11. Prostrate (pros TRAYT)—To lie flat, face downward, to show humility, or reverence; also overcome with exhaustion or grief.
12. Provocative—Stimulating; arousing anger, interest, sexual desire. *A provocative dance.*
13. Propriety—(Pro Pry uh tee). The word means the quality of being appropriate proper; conventional standards of behaviour. *To observe community proprieties.*
14. Prolix—Long-winded; tiresomely wordy and dull. *A prolix lecturer.*
15. Providential (prov í den shul)—Lucky, opportune, miraculous, suggesting divine intervention. *A providential rescue.*
16. Protectorate (pro tek tuh rayt)—The word means a territory largely controlled by a stronger nation. *Aden was once a British protectorate.*
17. Pro forma—It is a commonly used word. Latin phrase meaning 'for the sake of form'.
18. Proclivity (pro cliv ítee)—Combination of a tendency and a habitual indulgence, usually towards something bad. *A proclivity for malicious gossip.*
19. Prophetic (pro fet ik)—Predicting the future. *A prophetic warning about inflation.*
20. Prorate (pro rate)—To divide proportionally. *To prorate profits.*

We must know that when we add the prefix 'pro' to a word we are imparting meanings of before, forward or forth.

17

WORDS ENDING WITH 'UDE'

Uncommon Ending

Here we will be discussing a group of helpful nouns and verbs ending in 'ude' – an ending not too common in English language. A person must learn the correct meaning, pronunciation and context of use before he uses these words in written script and speech.

1. Solicitude (sõ lis í túde)—concern; anxiety. *To show solicitude for a person's welfare.* This word must not be confused with 'solitude' which means being solitary, lone, single, sole.
2. Interlude (ín ter lúde)—an intervening space or event. *A musical interlude between the acts of play.*
3. Exude (èks údè)—to sweat out; hence to ooze out like sweat. *Some trees exude a sticky sap.*
4. Aptitude (ap' tì túde)—skill; potential ability. *He has a natural aptitude for acting.*
5. Protrude (prõ trõõd)—to project, stick out; to thrust forth. *Guns protrude from every point in war front.*
6. Vicissitude (vi sis i tude)—change of fortune; variation in circumstances. *The vicissitude of life.* There is another word 'verisimilitude' which means appearance of being true. Many persons confuse these two words which are completely different.
7. Intrude (in trõõd')—to barge in; to enter without leave or welcome. *To intrude in one's privacy.* This word is often

confused with 'interlude'. One must be careful while using these words.

8. Fortitude (for ti tùde)—courage; resolute endurance; strength of mind to bear pain or adversity. *Fortitude of the Everest expedition.*
9. Latitude (lat i tude)—liberty of action; freedom from narrow limits. *To allow students great latitude in choice of subjects.*
10. Delude (de lude)—to deceive; to mislead. *To delude oneself with false hopes.*
11. Preclude (pre klude)—to prevent; to impede. *Prison measures that preclude escape.*
12. Prelude (pre lude)—an introductory performance; especially in music, a strain or movement introducing the theme. Hence, by extension the foreshadowing of a coming event. *A prelude to disaster* (note the spellings of the last two words P-r-e-c-l-u-d-e and P-r-e-l-u-d-e.
13. Lassitude (las i tude)—weariness; lethargy. *To be overcome by lassitude.*
14. Obtrude (ob trōōd)—to thrust into undue prominence. *False notes that obtrude upon the harmony of the musical composition.*
15. Allude (a lùde')—to refer to indirectly. *To allude to a past event.*
16. Ineptitude (in ep ti tùde)—inappropriateness; unsuitability; silliness. *Ineptitude of the speaker's, remarks.*
17. Magnitude (mag ni tùde)—great size; immensity. *The magnitude of the plan.*
18. Seclude (se klood)—to isolate; to withdraw from others. *To seclude oneself from the world.*
19. Rectitude (rek ti tùde)—uprightness; undeviating adherence to moral standards. *A man of unquestioned rectitude.*
20. Plentitude (plen i tude)—abundunce; plentiful amount. *A plenitude of riches.*

SECLUDE

In this section we saw the words endings with 'ude'. Certain words like *solicitude-solitude; aptitude-attitude* must all be used with great care. 'Solicitude' is concern and 'solitude' is being alone; 'Aptitude' is skill and 'attitude' is way of thinking or behaving (it also means position of the body). One must understand all these complex spellings and the idea behind it before using them in the right context.

Verbs—Allied in Meanings

In this section we will deal with some useful verbs which are closely allied in meaning. Identify these verbs, their meanings, pronunciation and context of use.

1. Militate (mil i tate) – To have force or influence (usually against). *Obstacles that militate against success.*
2. Desecrate (es e krate)—To debase or profane; to treat with sacrilege. *To desecrate a shrine.*
3. Vituperate (vitu per ate)—To revile; to abuse with words. *To vituperate a political adversary*.

LACERATE

4. Lacerate (las er ate)—To tear or rend; to mangle. *To lacerate the skin* (figuratively, to afflict with grief).
5. Fulminate (ful mi nate)—To denounce in thundering tones. *To fulminate against evil.*
6. Devastate (dev as tate)—To lay waste; to revage. *Wars devastate the land.*
7. Expostulate (ex pos tu late)—To remonstrate; to reason earnestly with a person. *To expostulate with a reckless driver.*
8. Annihilate (a nī hi late)—To destroy completely; to reduce to nothing. *To annihilate the enemy.*
9. Castigate (cas ti gate)—To reprove severely.*To castigate an unruly schoolboy.* This word is often confused with 'castrate'.
10. Extirpate (ek stir pate)—To pull out by the roots; to eradicate. *To extirpate crime.* This word is often confused with words like exacerbate–make worse; exaggerate–makes seem greater or larger than it really is; exasperate–annoy; execrate–express loathing for; curse; exterminate–destroy utterly.
11. Alienate (ale ýen ate)—To estrange; to separate; to exclude from confidence. *To alienate one's friends.*
12. Excoriate (èks kõ rí ate)—To flay. *To excoriate a carcass.*
13. Incriminate (in crím í nate)—To connect or charge with a crime. *Findings incriminate a person.*
14. Berate (bè ratè)—To chide vehemently; to scold severely. *To berate a mischievous child.*
15. Retaliate (rè tãl í ate)—To return like for like; usually to return evil for evil. This word is often confused with reiterate which means say or do again or repeatedly.
16. Subjugate (sùb' ju gate)—To conquer or subdue. *To subjugate a nation.*
17. Decimate (dès' í mate)—Originally, to take away one, tenth, to destroy a large part of. *To decimate a people by disease.* This must be distinguished from words like desiccate–dry out moisture from; designate–appointed but not yet installed;

delicate–exquisite, not robust or strong; desecrate–violate the sanctity of.

18. Deprecate (dè prè kate)—To express earnest and regretful disapproval of, with the hope of the opposite. *To deprecate public display of bad manners.* There is a similar word– depreciate 'de pre shi ate' meaning make or become lower in value.
19. Equivocate (è kwiv o kate)—To say one thing and mean another; to use ambiguous language with intent to deceive. *To equivocate on controversial question.*

Hope the journey through this list of 'allied in meaning' verbs was exciting. Words like 'deprecate-depreciate' must be used with care. We see in the list that many words are allied in meaning like 'devastate-annihilate'. These words must be used judiciously to avoid any kind of errors in their use.

18

PROPER USAGE OF NOUNS

The word 'name' in Latin is *nomen*, from which is derived the word 'noun'. In this section we will be discussing some nouns and there proper usage.

1. Overture—Tentative proposal; Intimation of a willingness to negotiate terms. *To make diplomatic overtures*.
2. Deterrent (de têr′ ent)—Restraint or prevention of action as by fear of consequences. *A deterrent to aggression*
3. Verbiage (vur′ bí ij)—Wordless; unnecessary use of words; *His thought was lost in verbiage*.
4. Purport—meaning; main idea. *The purport of a speech*.
5. Detraction (de trak shun)—Slander; defamation; taking away from the good name of another. *Exposed to the detraction of his enemies*. 'Distraction'is a similar sounding noun which means something that draws away the attention. 'Destruction' is a similar sounding noun which means demolition, ruin, ruination. Such similar sounding nouns can lead to errors in written or spoken English.
6. Puerility—Childishness; silliness; immaturity; act of puerility.
7. Composure (kom põ zher)—Calmness; tranquillity; serenity. *A look of complete composure*.
8. Perspicuity (pur spí kù i tí)—Clearness of expression; the quality of being easily understood. *A literary style noted for its perspicuity*. This noun is often confused with 'promiscuity'. Both are nouns but their meanings are totally different.
9. Appellation—a name or title.

10. Rendition (ren dish' un)—Generally an artistic, dramatic or musical interpretation; also the performance itself. *A rendition of Beethoven's 9th symphony.*
11. Compilation (kom pí lã shun)—Collection (as in book form) of material from various documents or sources.
12. Abeyance (a bã ance)—Suspension; temporary suppression. *To hold in abeyance a decision or action.*
13. Increment (in' kre ment)—Increase; enlargement; addition. *An increment in property values.*
14. Odium (õ dí um)—Hatred; disgust; keen dislike; now, usually the state or fact of being hated. *Behaviour that exposed him to odium*. This word should not be confused with 'podium' which means a projecting base.
15. Exaction—Demand; requirement. *The exaction of a high duty on imports.* This word should not be confused with 'extraction' meaning take out or obtain by force/effort; lineage.
16. Concomitant (kon kom í tant)—That which accompanies or attends. *High prices are often the concomitant of a scarcity of goods.*
17. Symposium (sim põ zí um)—A published collection of opinions or comments on a particular subject; also a conference at which a subject is discussed.
18. Inequity (in ek' wí tí)—Injustice; unfairness. *The occasional inequity arising from bureaucratic rulings.*
19. Impetus (im' pe tus)—Driving energy; momentum; also, impulse; stimulus.
20. Solace (sõl ís)—Consolation; comfort in grief or trouble.
21. Magnification—Increase in size; enlargement of an object state or condition; hence exaggeration. *Suffer from a magnification of one's troubles.*
22. Preconception—Opinion formed in advance of accurate knowledge prejudice. *Judgement warped by a preconception.*

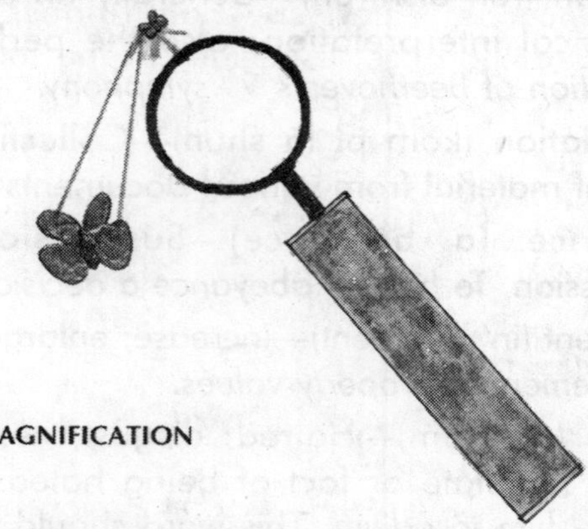
MAGNIFICATION

23. Compliance (kõm plí ans)—Consent; conformance; yielding to a demand. *Ready compliance with instruction*. Do not confuse it with complacent an adjective, meaning self satisfied; noun is complacency.
24. Fruition (froo ish un)—fulfilment; realisation. *To bring a plan to fruition.*
25. Affirmation (af er mã shun)—Solemn declaration; assertion. *An affirmation of loyalty*.
26. Premonition (prè mo nish'un)—Warning of something to come; presentiment. *A premonition of disaster*.
27. Commentary (note the spelling; *double* M)—Critical or explanatory remarks; treatise. *A commentary on advances in education.*
28. Abstinence (ab' stí nens)—Self-denial; self-control. *To practise total abstinence.*
29. Effusion (è fù 'zhun)—Unrestrained outpouring as of feelings; gushing utterance. *To speak with effusion*. There are certain similar sounding nouns: diffusion–'spreading widely or thinly'–a process; suffusion–a process of spreading throughout or over.
30. Assignment—Fixed task. *Handle a tough assignment*.
31. Repast (*rè past*)—meal. *A bountiful repast.*

32. Constancy (kon stan si)—Faithfulness; steadiness or firmness of purpose; especially in the face of difficulties. *The constancy of friends.*
33. Contour (kõn' toor)—Outline of a figure or body extended from sculpture to the outlines of coast, mountains, etc. *The contour of the land.*
34. Solicitation—Plea; petition; appeal. *A solicitation for contribution.*
35. Labyrinth (lãb` Ì rinth)—Bewildering maze of paths or passages; complicated or involved situation. *A labyrinth of red tape.*
36. Mediation – Intervention or intercession between disputing parties to bring agreement. *To settle a dispute by mediation*. Medication, meditation are similar sounding words.
37. Enterprise—Project, important undertaking. *To participate in a new enterprise.*
38. Qualification—Limitation, restrictive exception. *To accept without qualification*.
39. Annulment—Abolition; destruction of the force; validity or effect of as the annulment of a law.
40. Blemish—Imperfection; disfiguring mark or stain. *A character without blemish*.

After going through these 40 nouns, their meanings, pronunciations and correct contexts to use them the reader will feel confident. But the list does not end here. We have a large number of nouns which are often misused. Practice alone can make a person perfect enough to use nouns appropriately.

19

PUNCH WORDS

When a writer or a speaker wants to attract the attention of readers or listeners he uses words that pack a punch. While using such words one should avoid errors in meaning, context and of course the pronunciation. Given below are 20 such words that pack a punch. Learn and assimilate the meanings of these words and then use them without errors in the proper context.

1. Immobile (Ì moh bile)—Motionless; firmly placed. *The dog sat immobile listening to the music.*
2. Avuncular (ã vung kew ler)—like an uncle. *Avuncular advice is apt to be kindly and indulgent.*
3. Touchstone—A standard or criterion by which the genuineness of anything is measured. *The parliamentary system is a touchstone of democracy.* Two words to differentiate from Touchstone are Cornerstone – basis, vital foundation; and Tombstone – memorial stone set up over a grave.
4. Memoir (mem wah)—Biographical sketch, usually written by a friend or relative; highly personal autobiography.
5. Intermediate (in ter mee dee ut)—Situated or coming between two places or events. *An intermediate stage of the negotiations.*
6. Engrossed (en grow st)—Preoccupied. *To be engrossed in a story.*
7. Gelid (jel id)—very cold; frozen. *Gelid Arctic waters.*
8. Random—without prearranged order, plan or aim. *They bombed the area at random.* This word sounds like tandem, bicycle for two people one behind another.

MEMOIR
(Here it may be the personal experience of a doctor)

Calligraphy, Calligraphic
(to do with beautiful handwriting)

9. Sheepish—Embarrassed through shame. *To look sheepish after dropping a catch.*
10. Waggle—To wobble, move with short, quick motions. *She waggled her finger in warning.*
11. Acidulous (as ã sid yew lus)—slightly sour; also somewhat sarcastic. *The comedians stare of acidulous contempt.*
12. Burly—Sturdy, big and strong. *A burly policeman.*
13. Putative (pew tuh tive)—Supposed; reputed; commonly regarded as such. *Her putative ancestor was a queen.*
14. Calligraphic (cal Ì graff ik)—Having to do with beautiful handwriting, especially as an art.
15. Functionary—An official; someone acting in an official capacity.
16. Shenanigans (shí nan Ì ganz)—Mischievous nonsense; questionable or deceitful behaviour. *The shenanigans of naughty school children*.
17. Personable—Attractive, having a pleasing appearance or manner. *A personable young man.*
18. Courtly—Dignified, elegant. *The courtly older man charmed everyone* (not to be confused with curtly–rudely brief).
19. Pluck—Courage, fortitude. *The fireman's pluck saved many people.*

20. Confabulation—Informal or familiar conversation; conference. *A hurried confabulation among the delegates.*

Sense or Nonsense?

Verbs are the kingpins of language. The right verbs in the right places give life to our speech. We often come across them in the wrong places and then they turn our sentences into nonsense. Given below are 20 such verbs with their proper meaning, pronunciation and usage in the proper context.

1. Perturb (per turb')—to upset; to disturb; to trouble. *Youth problems perturb the community.*
2. Usurp (ù surp')—to seize power or position illegally. *To usurp the leadership of council.*
3. recriminate (rè krim Ì nate)—to accuse in return; to make a countercharge; to retort sharply or bitterly. *To recriminate against detractors.* This word should be differentiated from a similar word 'discriminate' means make a distinction (between), differentiate, distinguish.
4. Ensconce (en skons)—to settle comfortably or snugly. *To ensconce oneself before the fire.*
5. Elude (e lude)—to evade or avoid; to escape from. *To elude one's pursuers.* This word should be differentiated from *'delude'* means deceive.
6. Rifle—To plunder, ransack or pillage; to search through and rob. *To rifle a handbag* (as a noun this means a gun and a long-rifled barrel; as a verb it also means to cut spiral grooves in a gun barrel).
7. Mollify (mol Ì fí)—to appease; to pacify. *To mollify an angry crowd.*
8. recoup (rè koop')—to recover; to regain as compensation to make up for. *To recoup one's losses.*
9. Substantiate (sub stan' shi ãte)—To verify; to establish by strong proof. *To substantiate earlier statements.*
10. Solicit (sõ li's it)—To ask for; to try to obtain by request. *To solicit favours.*

11. Embroil (em broil')—To involve in dissension or strife. *To embroil the opposition in violent argument.*

12. Envisage (en vi zij)—To foresee or contemplate in imagination. *To envisage a bright future.*

13. Compound (Kom pound')- to put together, as elements or parts to form a whole; To combine. *To compound a prescription.*

14. Beguile (bè gilè) – to charm; to divert; to entertain. *To beguile the reader.* Beguile can also mean to delude, deceive or cheat.

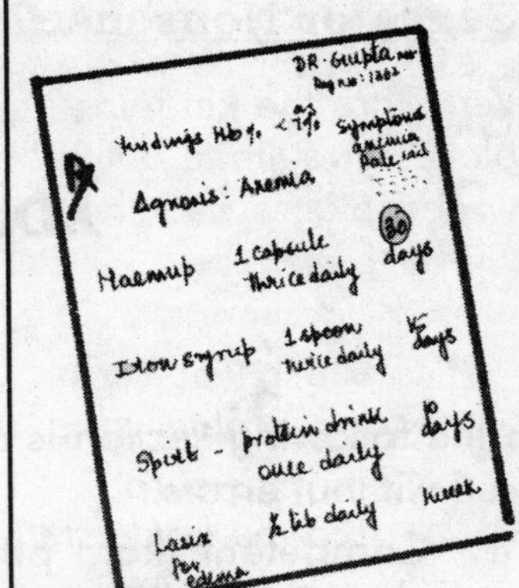

Compound
Ex.: To compound a prescription.

15. Slacken—To become less active or violent; to abate; to slow; to moderate. *To slacken one's pace.*

16. Submerge—To sink as in water; to cover or bury. *To submerge vital problems in political debate.*

17. Replenish (re plen ish)—To provide a new supply. *To replenish the larder.*

18. Convulse (kon vuls) – To shake violently; to agitate violently; to throw into confusion. *Periodic crises convulse the modern world.*

19. Placate (plã 'kate)—to pacify; to soothe. *To placate an opponent.*

20. Ingratiate (in grã shi ate)—To place (oneself) in a favourable position; to win confidence or favour. *He strove to ingratiate himself with the direction.*

20

ADJECTIVES

In the following section is a list of useful adjectives that can be used without errors.

1. Competent (kom pit ent)—Capable, adequate, having requisite qualifications. *A competent doctor*.
2. Analogous (a naÌ o gus)—Similar; resembling in certain respects; comparable. *A judicial system analogous to that of Britain*.
3. Erudite (è roo dite)—Learned; scholarly; having extensive knowledge. *An erudite teacher*.
4. Photogenic (foh toh jen' ik)—Eminently suitable for being photographed, especially from the aesthetic point of view. *A photogenic profile*.
5. Arduous (ah' dew us)—Difficult; demanding great effort; strenuous. *An arduous climb*.
6. Furtive (fur tiv)—Stealthy; sly and evasive; surreptitious. *A furtive glance*.
7. Radiant (ray' dí ant)—Glowing; expressing light, joy, love, hope. *A radiant face*.
8. Mettlesome (met Ì sum)—Spirited; full of mettle or spirit; fiery. *A mettlesome horse*. Meddlesome is an adjective meaning 'often interfering in people's affairs. Do not get confuse as both these adjectives sound similar.
9. Primal (pry' mal)—primitive; original. *Primal villages*; also first in importance; fundamental. *A primal necessity*.

**Note the usage: She has a radiant face.
She has a photogenic profile.**

10. Colossal (ko los' al)—Huge, enormous. *A colossal industrial complex.*
11. Bumptious (bump' shus)—Offensively and often noisily self assertive. *A bumptious crowd of demonstrators.*
12. Amiable (aim l able)—Friendly; pleasant; lovable. *An amiable character.* There is a similar word amicable, which also means 'friendly'; Amiable has many more meanings. It means likeable, affable, agreeable, charming, cordial, genial, good natured, kind, kind hearted, kindly, pleasant. One of the meanings of amiable is amicable.
13. Diabolic (dye a bol ik)—fiendish, extremely wicked; devilish. *A diabolic hijacking plot.*
14. Ethical (eth i kal)—Moral; pertaining to accepted standards of right and wrong. *Ethical medical practices.*
15. Callous (kal' us)—Insensitive, unfeeling, hardened. *Callous blackmailers.*
16. Illimitable—Boundless; without limit; measureless. *Illimitable space.*
17. Inexorable (in ek' so rab 'l) Unyielding; relentless. *The inexorable march of time.*
18. Lucrative (loo' kra tiv)—Highly profitable, producing wealth; money making. *A lucrative job.*
19. Vindictive (vin dik' tiv)—Vengeful; vicious; spiteful; malicious. *A vindictive attack.*

20. Raucous (raw' kus)—Disagreeably harsh or strident; hoarse. *The raucous call of crows*.

While using the above adjectives for description care must be taken to use the appropriate adjective in the appropriate context.

Why so much importance is being given to pronunciation? The following episode not only brings out the wonderful and fanciful nature of English language but also clarifies the importance of pronunciation being proper and clear to express a sensible statement.

An eccentric chap named Turner recently began signing his name *phtholognyrrh*. People were surprised, puzzled and shocked by this name. Pressed for an explanation, he justified his bizarre orthography as follows.

Phth as in Phthisic is pronounced T.

Olo, as in colonel is pronounced UR.

Gn as in gnat is pronounced N.

Yrrh as in myrrh is pronounced ER.

As a cursory glance the above explanation may sound funny but on delving deeply we can understand how pronunciation of syllables is distinct in each word and how profound the concept of pronunciation is.

One must pay great care in proper pronunciation of words to clarify a thought or expression.

21

POSITION OF VERBS AND ADJECTIVES

VERBS

The verb is the hinge upon which many an effective sentence swings, says author Charles Ferguson. But verbs used in the wrong places will make one's sentences creak. Forty such verbs often used in wrong places due to ignorance of its meaning are discussed in this section.

1. Nurture—To nourish; to care for and train. *To nurture the sapling in the garden.*

Nurture: a plant

2. Abridge—To shorten; to cut off; to curtail. *To abridge a long manuscript.*
3. Disinter—To dig up, as from the grave; to exhume. *To disinter a body for autopsy.*
4. Immure—to enclose, as within walls; hence, to shut up to imprison. *To immure rioting convicts.*

5. Renounce—To give up entirely, to disclaim. *To renounce one's ambitions.*
6. Affix—To fasten on; to attach. *To affix blame.*
7. Amend—To improve, by freeing from errors. *To amend a law.*
8. Impart—To share with another; to reveal; to make known. *Jesus used parables to impart his teachings.*
9. Brandish—To wave in a threatening way; to flourish defiantly. *To brandish a weapon.*
10. Impair—To weaken, to cause to become less or worse. *To impair health.*
11. Diverge—to spread apart; to lead away from each other. *Their careers began to diverge.*
12. Seethe—To be violently agitated; to foam as in boiling. *To seethe with hatred.*
13. Emit—To utter; to voice, to give out. *To emit an oath.*
14. Append—to add to or attach as supplementary material. *To append notes to a book.*
15. Pertain—To relate, to have reference; to concern. *To pertain to another subject.*
16. Confer—To bestow or grant to give. *To confer an honorary degree.*
17. Converge—To move towards one point; to come together gradually. *The two roads converge.* The word converse, as a verb means talk; as an adjective it means opposite or contrary).
18. Illuminate—To light up; to enlighten; to make bright and clear. *To illuminate the path ahead.*
19. Decoct—to extract the properties of by boiling. *To decoct a medicinal essence from herbs/seeds.*
20. Cannon—To bounce off after striking, as a ball from a billiard cushion. *To see a car canon off a wall.* The noun canon means member of cathedral clergy; general rule or principle; set of writing accepted as genuine. One should not get confused between cannon (verb) and canon (noun).

21. Impose—To inflict; to levy; to lay as a charge, penalty obligation. *To impose a tax.*
22. Misappropriate—To take and use dishonesty. *To misappropriate funds.*
23. Inter—To bury, as a body.
24. Discount—To allow you exaggeration; to give less than full credit. *To discount his story.*
25. Defer—To postpone; to delay. *To defer judgement.* There is another verb 'deter' which means prevent; discourage from action. One must not get confused between these two verbs.
26. Speculate—To ponder; to meditate or reflect. *To speculate on the enemies' plans.*
27. Subsist—to stay alive; to exist. *To subsist is not to live.*
28. Default—To fail in an obligation or duty. *To default on a contract.*
29. Belabour—To thrash or beat soundly; hence to assail verbally. *To belabour one's opponent.*
30. Salvage—To rescue or save from waste, wreckage or destruction. *To salvage scrap metal.*
31. Burnish—To polish; to make shiny by rubbing. *To burnish brass.*
32. Compose—to adjust, as a dispute; to arrange or settle. *To compose our difficulties.*
33. Meander—To wander aimlessly. *To meander through the garden.*
34. Embellish—To decorate; to adorn; to beautify by adding ornamental features. *To embellish a book with engravings.*
35. Amplify—To elaborate; to enlarge upon a statement. *To amplify one's remarks.*
36. Abide—To stand firm by; to hold to; to remain true to. *To abide by the rules.*
37. Bolster—To support, to prop up. *To bolster public confidence.*

38. Revel—To take keen delight, satisfaction or pleasure (in). *To revel in new found glory.*
39. Protract—To prolong; to lengthen. *To protract a debate.*
40. Adhere—to hold firmly and loyally; to cling. *To adhere to one's principles.*

Adjectives

An adjective means 'added to'. Adjectives are added to a noun to enlarge its meaning and to limit its use. The following list gives stress to these two points.

1. Conclusive—Convincing; decisive; final; dispelling all doubt. *A conclusive evidence.*
2. Conformable—in agreement; harmonious. *A diet conformable to the rules of health.*
3. Spectral—Ghostly; ghostlike. *A spectral gloom.* This word is often confused with several similar sounding words like speckle, spectacle, spectre, spectrum and speculum.
4. Susceptible—Capable of being affected; easily influenced. *A gentle person susceptible to criticism.*
5. Estimable—Worthy of high regard, deserving esteem. *An estimable citizen.*
6. Bilingual—Speaking two languages. *A bilingual person.*
7. Accessory—aiding in a subordinate way; additional supplementary. *Accessory equipment.*
8. Tangible—Definite, real; literally capable of being touched, felt. *Tangible benefits.*
9. Distraught—greatly excited; under intense stress. *A distraught accident victim.*
10. Exorbitant—Excessive; extravagant; going beyond proper limits. *An exorbitant price.*
11. Misanthropic—Hating mankind; distrusting and avoiding human beings. *A misanthropic recluse.*
12. Obligatory—In the nature of a duty, morally binding. *Obligatory commitments.*

13. Unwarranted—Unjustifiable; not defensible, unauthorised. *Unwarranted criticism.* Note the spelling U-n-w-a-r-r-a-n-t-e-d. This word is not to be confused with unwanted (U-n-w-a-n-t-e-d), meaning not customary not usual).
14. Sumptuous—Luxurious, costly, magnificent. *A sumptuous repost.*
15. Jaded—Worn out; wearied; wanted in zest. *A jaded appetite.*
16. Valid—Supported by authority; effective; lawfully binding. *A valid decree.*
17. Vitriolic—Sharp and biting, caustic; severely critical; like a strong acid which burns and scars. *Vitriolic criticism.*
18. Intuitive – Instinctive, gained from within and not through experience. *An intuitive understanding of people.*
19. Derogatory—Belittling; expressive of disdain detracting from good repute. *A derogatory statement.*
20. Statuesque—Having the dignity and quietude of a statue. *A statuesque figure.*

Adjectives have been called the seasoning of words! When they are precisely used, they add colour and force to speech and writing. It is often seen that adjectives are misused. This misuse includes overuse and underuse. They need to be used very precisely. This section lists several adjectives, with their meaning and proper contexts of their use.

1. Banal (banal; ba' nahl')—Commonplace; trite; flat. *A banal remark.*
2. Trenchant (tren' chãnt)—Incisive, penetrating; sharp and clear; A trenchant argument. It also means keen mentally energetic. *A Trenchant critic.*
3. Frugal (froo gal)—Economical; avoiding waste; saving. *A frugal housewife.*
4. Arduous (ar du us)—Difficult; involving great labour or hardship. *Arduous campaign.*
5. Nominal (nõm' I níl)—Too small or slight to be considered; virtually nothing; existing in name only. *A nominal price.*

6. Tolerant (tõÌ er' ant)—Forbearing; indulgent. *Tolerant of one's misbehaviour.*
7. Dubious (dù bí ùs)—doubtful; uncertain. *A plan of dubious value.*
8. Sedentary (sed' en tri)—Characterised by, or requiring, sitting. *A sedentary job.* Also accustomed to sit much or long. *A sedentary person.*
9. Plebeian (plè bè ãn)—common; inferior; vulgar pertaining to the common people. *Plebeian custom.*
10. Sophisticated (sõ fí tí kãt èd)—Worldly-wise; lacking in simplicity. *Sophisticated view pont.*
11. Obese (õ bès)—excessively fat; corpulent. *An obese figure.*
12. Lethargic (*lè thar' jik*)—Drowsy; dull; inactive. *A lethargic audience.*
13. Lucrative—Highly profitable; productive of wealth. *A lucrative business.*
14. Garish (gar' ish)—Unpleasantly guady; showy; flashy. *She was wearing a garish costume.*
15. Tawny—Brownish yellow; of the colour or things tanned. *A tawny coat.*
16. Vibrant (vi' brant)—Quivering, vibrating, thrilling with. *Vibrant tones.*
17. Rhetorical (rè tõ ri kãl)—Designed for showy oratorical effect; artificial. *A speech punctuate by rhetorical flight.*
18. Dispassionate (dis pash' ùn ãt)—Calm; unbiased; impartial. *A dispassionate analysis.*
19. Definitive (dè fin Ì tiv)—Conclusive; sharply defined; final; complete. *A definitive biography.*
20. Sagacious (sã gã shùs)—Discerning; farsighted in judgement; keenly perceptive; shrewd. *A sagacious parent.*
21. restive (res' tív)—restless; uneasy; fidgety. *The crowd grew restive.*

22. Craven (krã 'ven)—Cowardly; full of fear. *A craven attitude.*
23. Deferential (dèf er en' shãl)—Respectful; having regard for the opinion or wishes of another. *A deferential manner.*
24. Inchoate—In an elementay stage; recently begun; rudimentary. *An inchoate civilisation.*
25. Usurious (ù zhoor íus)—Pertaining to high interest or usurious rates – for use of money.
26. Discursive (dis kur' sív)—Rambling; digressive; shifting from one subject to another. *A discursive speech.*
27. Grandiose (gran di os)—Impressive, imposing, pompous. *A grandiose gesture.*
28. Inviolate (in vi o late)—Pure, unbroken, unimpaired. *An inviolate right.*
29. Implicit (im plís' it)—understood; though not specifically stated; implied; as an implicit agreement; also by transference; unquestioning; complete. *Implicit faith* (Explicit–This adjective means stated plainly or clear, categorical, definite. Often a person gets confused between explicit and implicit. They are opposites and one must be careful in using them.)
30. Athwart (a thwort')—crosswise; across. *A shadow lay athwart the path.*
31. Gargantuan (gar gan' tu an)—Gigantic; huge. *A gargantuan task.*
32. Portentous—Ominous; threatening. *A portentous sign.*
33. Secular (sèk ù lar)—Worldly; referring to temporal rather than spiritual affairs. *Secular school.*
34. Extraneous—External or foreign; pertaining to that which is outside. *Extraneous influence.*
35. Dogmatic (dog mat' ik)—Excessively opinionated; unduly positive in manner or speech. *A dogmatic peacher.*
36. Furtive (fur' tív)—Stealthy; sly; secret like the action of a

thief. *A furtive glance. Not to be confused* with fugitive (noun)–person who is fleeing or escaping; Fugitive(adj)–fleeing, transient.

37. Copious (kõ pí us)—Abundant; ample; plentiful. *A copious supply.*
38. Sentient (sen' shent; - shí ent)—Capable of feeling and sensation. *A sentient feeling.* There is a similar sounding word sentiment. This noun means mental feeling, opinion.
39. Insatiable (in sã shí ab'l; sha b'l)—Greedy; not capable of being satisfied. *An insatiable appetite.*
40. Stentorian (sten tor' Ì an)—Extremely loud; loud voiced. *Stentorian tones.*

22

FOWLERISMS AND RED TYPE WORDS

Fowlerisms

Although Henry Fowler died over 60 years ago, his modern English usage is still an indispensable reference book for all who value the correct use of the language. In this section we will be discussing 20 words on which Fowler's classic work gives guidance.

1. Affinity—Relationship between two mutually benefiting parties. *The affinity between Britain and the USA.*
2. Aftermath—Unpleasant consequence. *As war and its aftermath;* literally grass growing after the first growth has been mown.
3. Bereft—deprived. Are you bereft of your sense.
4. Complacency (kom play sen see)—Self-satisfaction. *Britain unemployment figures leave no room for complacency.*
5. Demean—To lower or debase. *I would not demean myself to speak to him.*
6. Egregious (Ì gree jus)—Shocking; outstandingly bad. *An egregious example of incapacity.*
7. Epnoymous—Named after a person; as the words boycott (after captain C.C. Boycott), guillotine (Dr. J.J. Guillotin); Sandwich (the fourth earl).
8. Fortuitous—Accidental. *A fortuitous encounter.*
9. Idiosyncrasy—Individuality; the mixtures of characteristics that makes each of us unique.
10. Innate—Inborn. *Courage is innate in the race.*

11. Jetsam—Goods thrown overboard to lighten a ship and subsequently washed ashore.
12. Lampoon—Satirical article written to abuse an individual.
13. Meander (meen an der)—To wander or follow a winding course. *A meandering river.*
14. Mendacity (men DAS it ee)—Untruthfulness. *A criminal's habitual mendacity.*
15. Oblivious—Forgetful; no longer aware. *To become oblivious of worldly cares.*
16. Plausible (plaw zí b'l) – Persuasive, but deceptively so. *A plausible liar.*
17. Prolific—Highly productive. *A prolific writer.*
18. Straiten—To restrict in range or scope. *Straitened circumstances.*
19. Supine—Lying face upwards. *Supine figures of sunbathers.*

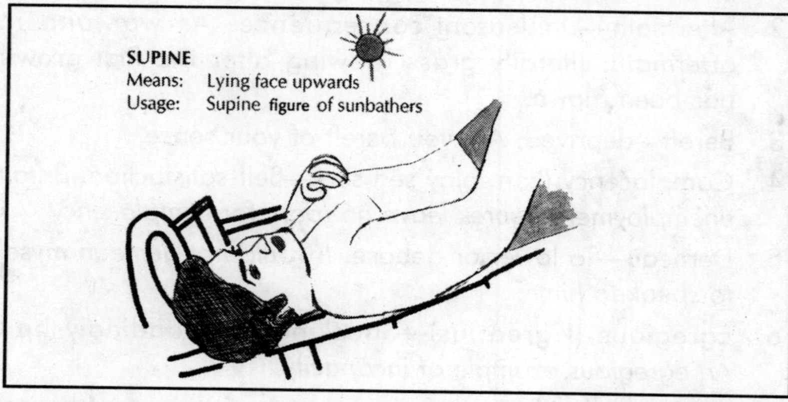

20. Venial—Excusable; not very wrong. *The venial fault of absentmindedness.*

Fowler's classic work has given guidance on the abovementioned 20 words. Every word has a distinct meaning and contextual use. If one misuses them it can lead to an error in speech or written scripts. So be careful.

Red Tape Words

We come across the following words in news channels, newspapers and in magazines. Often due to ignorance of meaning and contextual use these words are either not understood or are misunderstood. Subsequently when used it is prone to error. One has to be well trained in the use of these words to get over these red tape word. This section lists 20 such words.

1. Ally—Partner or associate; country or group joined with another for a common purpose.
2. Revelation—Disclosure of knowledge and revealed in a striking way.
3. Allegation—An uproven statement or assertion, especially an accusation.
4. Modus operandi—Way of working, procedure.
5. Insurgency—Revolt; uprising.
6. Pragmatism—Quality of being; matter of fact and realistic as opposed to theoretical; officiousness.
7. Entente Cordiale—Friendly understanding among nations in regard to foreign affairs.
8. Doctrinaire—Theoretical and unpractical; person who applies principle without regard to practical difficulties.
9. Imperialism—Empire building; policy by a country to dominate weaker nations through trade diplomacy.
10. Occidental—Of the west; not to be confused with accidental, meaning, happening by accident.
11. Protocol—Code or rules of diplomatic etiquette and procedure.
12. Extradite—To hand over an alleged criminal for trial to another country or state.
13. Recitation—A public delivery of prose or poetry learnt by heart. Not to be confused with rendition—the way something is performed.
14. Mediation—Friendly intervention by a neutral power to bring about a peaceful settlement of a dispute between nations.

15. Status quo—Existing condition.
16. Incommunicado—Unable or not allowed to communicate with other people or the outside world.

Extradite

17. Reprisal—Retaliation; revenge.
18. Cosmopolitan—Wordly; belonging to many or all parts of the world.
19. Besmirch—To sully; soil.
20. De' marche—Diplomatic manoeuvre or initative; a political step.

23

ONE WORD, MANY USES

A few words can be used in many ways. Given below are some expressions with these words. Even knowledgeable persons often misuse these words. This section gives some idea on their use.

Set

1. Set something (off) against something—Consider something good or positive as balancing or outweighing something bad or negative. *Set against her virtues, her fault do not seem bad.*
2. Set something aside—Save or keep something (money or time) for a good purpose, also disregard, ignore, abandon or reject something. *We need to set aside our sentiments and think logically.*

He has set aside some money (as savings) for the rainy day.

3. Set something back (from something)—Place or situate something at a distance from something. *The hotel is set well back from the road.*
4. Set on someone—Attack someone; Cause an animal/ person to attack someone. *The farmer set his dogs on us.*

5. Set (oneself) up as someone—establish oneself in some business; also regard oneself as a specified kind or person. *He likes to set himself up as an intellectual.*

Brush

1. Brush someone/something off—Push someone or something to one side; pay little or no attention to some on something. *He is keen on her but she is always brushing him off.*
2. Brush against/by/past someone/something—Touch someone or something lightly while moving close to him/her.
3. Brush something up/brush up on something—Study or practise something in order to get back a knowledge or skill that was lost. *I must brush up my French before I leave for Paris.*
4. Brush something away/off—Remove something (from something) with a brush, or as if with a brush. *Mud brushes off easily when it is dry.*

Fob

(i) Fob off (Fob something off)—Trick someone into buying or accepting something interior. *He tried to fob off stale vegetables on us.*

(ii) Fob someone off—Trick someone into being satisfied. *I am a diamond expert, so do not fob me off with cheap stones.*

Face

1. Face up to something—Accept and deal with something that is unpleasant/demanding in a brave and honest manner. *He must face up to the fact that he is no longer young.*
2. Till one is blue in the face—Do something as hard and as long as one possibly can. *He can justify his action till he is blue in the face but I am not going to believe a word.*

3. Grind the faces of the poor—Deliberately cause poor people to suffer more than necessary. *Take pleasure in doing so.*
4. Not just a pretty face—Not someone who is just superficially attractive without having any other quality. *His good looks won him the election but he has still to prove that he is not just a pretty face.*

24

THE ACTION STATION

Verbs are the 'dynamos' of a language. Nobody can get along without them. This section presents a list of 40 verbs with meanings, pronunciation and context of use.

1. Adjudicate (ã joo dí kate)—To determine judicially; to settle by judicial decree; to act as judge. *To adjudicate on who is to get the prize.*
2. Inveigle (in ve g'l; in va g'l)—To lead on by deceit; to delude; to ensnare or win over by guile. *To inveigle a witness into a damaging admission.*
3. Exculpate (eks' kul pate)—To free from blame; to clear from alleged fault or guilt. *To exculpate a suspect.*
4. Portray—To depict; to make a picture of; to describe in words. *To portray a fascinating character.*
5. Incense (in sens')—To enrage; to inflame with anger. *To incense a political opponent.*
6. Incarcerate (in kar' ser ate)—To imprison; to put in jail.
7. Rescind (rè sínd')—To repeal or abrogate; to make void. *To rescind a law.*
8. Obfuscate (ob' fus kate)—To confuse; to bewilder; to obscure. *To obfuscate the issue.*
9. Cavil (kãv íl)—To find fault; to carp; to raise frivolous objections. *To cavil at the terms of a contract.*
10. Enthral (en thrawl')—To captivate; to fascinate. *To enthral an audience with music.*

11. Regale (re gale')—To entertain prodigally; to give delight to. *To regale friends with a sumptuous meal.*
12. Inculcate (in' kul kate)—To impress upon the mind by repetition to instill; to teach. *An effort to inculcate respect for law.*
13. Confiscate (kon' fis kate)—To seize, often by governmental authority, as a penalty. *To confiscate stolen property.*
14. Evince (è víns')—To show plainly; to make evident. *To evince interest in the plan.*
15. Inveigh (in vã)—To rail; to attack with angry words. *To inveigh against pop music.*
16. Entrance (en trans)—To charm; to fill with rapture and wonder. *A play certain to entrance children.* Another word is enthral which means which hold spellbound. Both Entrance and Enthral have similar meanings. Entrance as a noun means a door or passage by which one enters; act or instance of entering; right of admission, fee for this. *Entrance examination for medical college; entrance fee for the show.*
17. Evoke—To call forth or summon. *To evoke nostalgic recollection.*
18. Deploy (de ploy)—To spread out in extended formation. *To deploy troops.*

19. Ostracise (ōs trā size)—To exclude from a group by common consent; to banish. *To ostracise known agitators.*
20. Perpetrate (per pe trate)—To perform; execute or carry through; also, to be guilty of. *To perpetrate a crime.*
21. Appease (ā pèz')—To pacify; to calm; to soothe; to satisfy; to conciliate. *An attempt to appease the hot heads.*
22. Acquiesce (ak wí es)—To accept or comply tacitly or passively without active opposition. *Her parents will never acquiesce in such an unsuitable marriage.*
23. Detonate (dèt' o nate)—To explode or cause to explode. *To detonate a charge of dynamite.*

24. Ransack (ran' sack)—To search thoroughly; to rummage; to explode. *To ransack one's room.*
25. Enjoin (en join')—To forbid; to prohibit (by law). *Enjoin obedirence on followers.*
26. Repudiate (re pù dí ate)—To reject or disclaim; to disown; to renounce. *To repudiate a treaty.*
27. Foment (fo ment')—To stir up; to instigate. *To foment a riot.* A similar word is 'ferment'—stir up, excite.
28. Preempt (prè emp't)—To appropriate; to take possession of to the exclusion of others. *To preempt the best seat.*
29. Burgeon (bur jun)—To send forth buds or shoots; to sprout hence to show signs of life. *A hope that burgeons in the heart.*

30. Expunge (eks punj)—To blot; to obliterate. *To expunge any thought of failure.*
31. Culminate (kul mi nate)—To reach a fual effect; to attain the highest point or degree. *Effort that culminates in success.*
32. Appertain (ap er tane)—To belong to by right; association or fitness. *Laws that appertain to commerce.*
33. Countenance—To encourage by showing approval; to favour; to sanction. *To countenance early marriages.*
34. Covet (kùv' et)—To desire eagerly; to long for especially something belonging to another. *A nation that covet another nation's markets.* Not to confuse with covert means a thick undergrowth where animals hide; covert (adjective) means done secretly.
35. Elicit—to draw forth; to evoke; *To elicit a reply.* Illicit means unlawful, illegal. *Illicit relationship; Illicit liquor.*
36. Dally—To trifle or play with. *To dally with another's affections.*
37. Proliferate (pro lif er ate)—To produce frequently; to reproduce; especially with rapidity. *Government rules and regulations proliferate.*
38. Concoct (kõn kõkt)—To prepare or make up. *To concoct an appetising stew or figuratively to concoct an excuse.*
39. Denominate (dè nõm Ì nate)—To name; to designate. *To denominate a successor.* Dominate means having a commanding influence over, while nominate means propose as a candidate; appoint to an office; designate.
40. Arraign (ã ranè)—To call to account; to accuse specifically, to call (a prisoner) before a court to answer a charge. *Arraigned for theft.*

In the above section we have discussed 40 verbs, their meanings, pronunciation and context of use. One should be careful in using these verbs. They should be used in appropriate places. They are 'action stations' and need proper usage. An improper use of verbs can lead to serious errors in sentences, speech and expressions.

Word Processor

In this section are given some words chosen at random to show how they should be used without mistakes.

1. Cleave—The word occurs in two separate forms with different origins and with virtually opposite meanings. Split or break apart; Stick or adhere. One should be very careful using this word as it can convey two different meanings which are not substitutes for one another. It is interesting to know that in modern German the two words are very similar: Klieben – to split; Kleben – to stick.

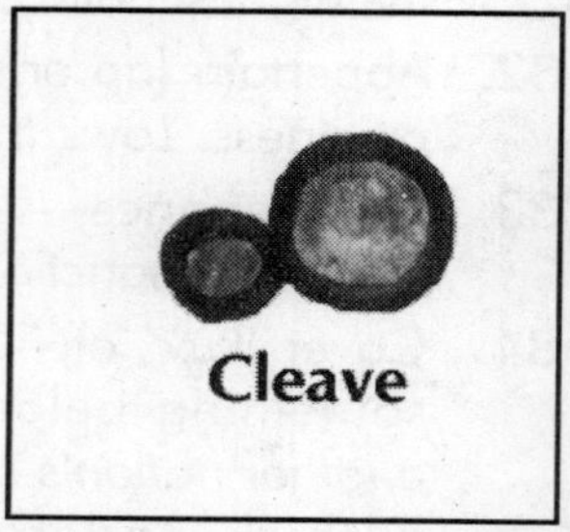

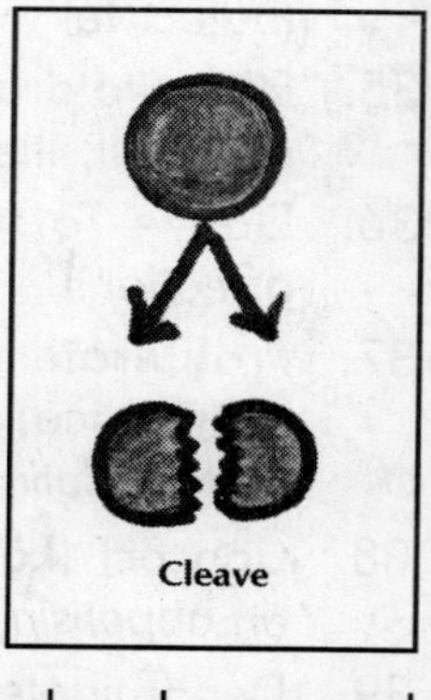

2. Quarantine—Any forced stoppage of travel or communication on account of malignant contagious disease on land or by sea. From the French *quarante* (forty), adding the suffix *aine* to French numbers gives a degree of roughness to the figure (like *ish* in English). This word is often mispronounced and one need to be cautious while using this word in speech.
3. Phoney—British thieves and swindlers of old used many secret code words. One such word was *fawney* which referred to a gilt ring. They would sell these, saying that they were made of real gold, but the rings were not genuine gold and the word *phony* from *fawney* came to be used for anything that was fake or not genuine. Understanding the origin of such words helps one to use these words with better sense.
4. Inveigle—The word inveigle has two closely related senses that have to do with accomplishing something through artful talk. The first is "to entice or lure through artful talk

or inducement", and the second is " to obtain by beguiling talk or methods".

5. Toothsome—One meaning of 'tooth' is a fondness or taste for something specified, a liking. Toothsome comes from this definition of tooth plus the suffix. Some meaning characterised by toothsome was first used to describe general attractiveness. It quickly developed a second sense that was specific to the sense of taste (perhaps because from as far back as Chaucer's time, 'tooth' could also refer specifically to eating). In addition "Toothsome" is now showing signs of acquiring a third sense, 'toothy' (as in a "toothsome grin"). But this sense is not yet established to qualify for dictionary entry. One has to be careful in using this word and must keep is mind the above facts to avoid errors in the usage of this word.
6. Peccadillo—A slight or trifling offence. "The world loves a spice of wickedness". That observation by Henry Wadsworth Longfellow may explain why people are willing to forgive peccadilloes as foolishness or lapses of judgement. English speakers borrowed a modified version of the Spanish *pecadillo* in the late 1500s. The Spanish distinguished the peccadillo or little sun from the more serious '*pecado*' the term for a sin of magnitude, but in Spain their words can be traced back to the Latin verb *peccare* meaning 'to sin'.
7. Scapegoat—Originally it was a Biblical reference, to Leviticus 16. The scapegoat was a goat let loose in the wilderness on Yom Kippur after the high priest symbolically laid the sins of the people on its head. The usual sense now, "a person or group made to bear the blame for other or to suffer in their place", is a figurative use. The word was coined by William Tyndale, an English religious reformer, in his influential translation of the *Bible* in 1530. Tyndale formed scapegoat from scape an obsolete form of escape, and goat with the word thus meaning "the goat that departs".

8. News—The original sense of news was "new things"; this is long obsolete. Since the fifteenth century it has been used to mean tidings, the report of recent events, new occurrences as a subject or report or talk. The objective now goes back to old English. Anybody using this word must know its meaning, otherwise the expression is bound to be used in the wrong context.
9. Bootleg—The original meaning of the word bootleg in the seventeenth century was: the upper part of a boot, as the people used to smuggle liquor by hiding the hooch in their boots. Strange as this may seem it was apparently a real practice in the late nineteenth century. Rather than phoniness or inauthenticity the main meaning is something like "Illegal; unauthorised; unregulated". The broader application to anything smuggled or made illicitly, such as bootleg cigarettes or a bootleg recording, arose by the 1920s.
10. Cancer—Both the disease and the astronomical constellation derive from the Latin *Cancer* or *Cancrum* meaning crab. The astrological sign of course is said to resemble a crab and the ancient Greek Physician Galen noted the similarity between a certain type of tumour with a crab as well. But despite a common origin, the two senses came into English via different routes. The name of the disease is older in English—cancer the disease dates to about the year 1,000. The astronomical sign was introduced into English about 1391 and appears in Chaucer. While using this word one cannot go wrong in the context as the two words are very distinct. Knowing the origin of the word, of course gives more meaning to its usage.

11. Flying colours—The original form appears to be "come off with flying colours". This dates to at least 1706. Many casually assume that the origin is naval but it is more likely military, being a reference to retiring from the battlefield with unit colours intact and flying. Now it is used to mean 'to excel in' something.

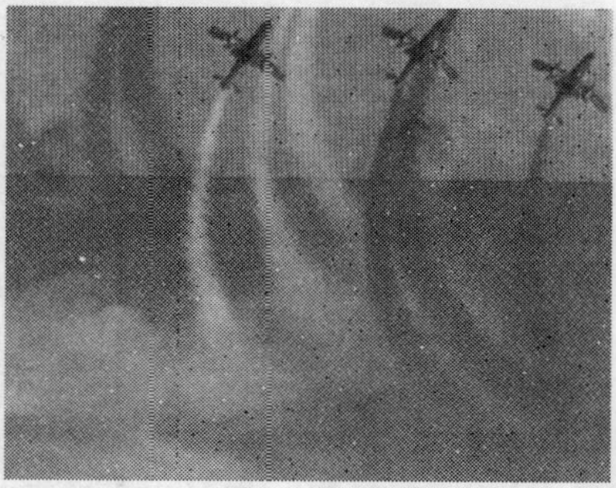

'come off with flying colours'-

25

SOUND OF WORDS

Part of the pleasure of speaking comes from the sound of words. Some words flow sonorously while others have an abrupt tone. The following section lists 20 words, each having an interesting or an unusual sound – resonant, pungent or amusing. While speaking one must keep this quality of words in mind. Pronunciation, meaning and context of use of these words are often prone to error. The section below gives the right use of these words.

1. Dilly-dally (dillee dall ee) – To dawdle; loiter; waste time by vacillating. *To dilly dally in making a decision.*
2. Namby-pamby (nah bí pah bí) – Weakly sentimental; without character. *Namby-pamby lyrics*. From a nick-name given to Ambrose Philips, eighteenth century poet whose verse was considered overly sentimental.
3. Perspicacity (per spi kass Ì tee) – Mental discernment. *The teacher displayed considerable perspicacity in separating the troublesome boy from his friends.*
4. Serendipity – An aptitude for making happy discoveries by accident. *Once again serendipity came to his aid as he bumped into the very man who could help him.* This term was coined by Horace Walpole in 1754 after a fairy tale called 'The Three Princes of Serendip'.
5. Scrumptious – Delicious. *A scrumptious casserole is very pleasing to taste*. Sumptuous is splendid and costly looking.

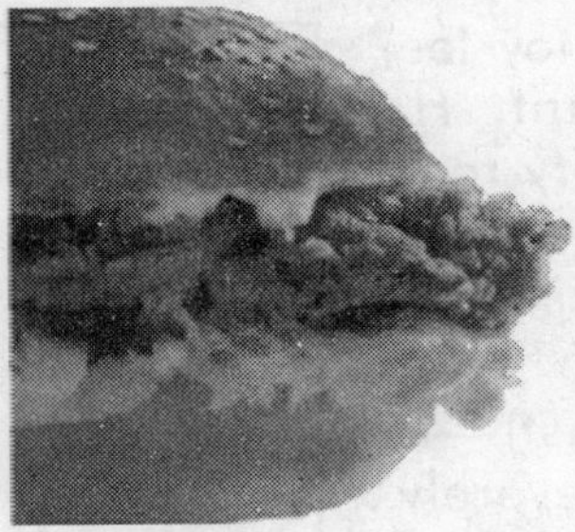

Scrumptious

6. Hoi polloi (hoy pol loy) – The majority; the masses; the rabble. *When the filmstar went out among the hoi polloi she needed five bodyguards for protection.*
7. Flabbergasted (flab er gas ted) – Astonished or amazed. *To be flabbergasted by some news.*
8. Smorgasbord (Smer gaz board) – Swedish hors d'oeuvres, buffet meal with a variety of dishes. Swedish *smor* (goose, butter) *gas*, table *bord*.
9. Rapscallion (rap skal yun) – Rascal, rogue, scoundrel. This word originated from the earlier *rascallion*.
10. Gabble (ga b'l)–To talk rapidly and unintelligibly, sounding like a goose; jabber, *He gabbled on and on about his misfortunes*. (This word is often used as synonym to blab talk indiscreetly).
11. Bumptious (bump shus)—Conceited or disagreeably self-assertive; pushy. *The bumptious newcomer sought to oust the committie's popular member*.
12. Hyperbole (hy per bol ee)—Exaggerated statement; not to be taken literally.
13. Smidgen (smij un)—A very small amount; tiny bit; trifle. *A smidgen of butter.*
14. Heyday—Peak or acme; the time of greatest vigour, success or power. *He was a football star in his hey day.*
15. Cornucopia (kor new koh pi ya)—Abundant supply. *The farmhouse larder was a positive cornucopia of home bottled fruits and home baked pies*.

16. Hoity-toity (hoy tee toy tee)—Haughty; petulant. *He became very hoity-toity when we pointed out his limousine was blocking our entrance.*

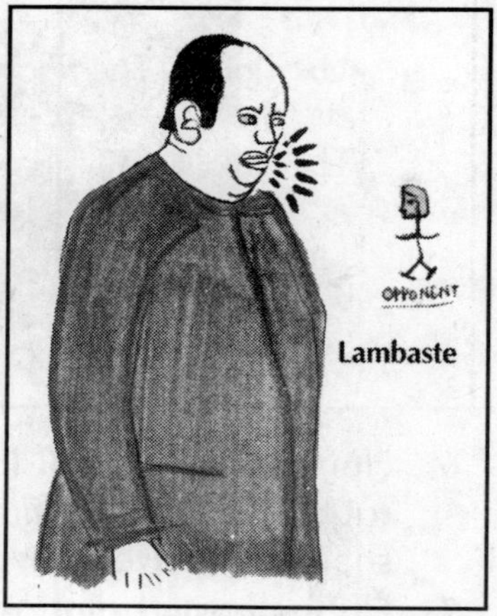

Lambaste

17. Lambaste (Lam bast)—To scold or criticise severely. *To lambaste an opponent also to beat or thrash.*
18. Riff-raff—The most disputable people in society; rabble; mob.
19. Spangle (spang g'l)—Small, bright sparkling object. *Her evening dress was covered with spangles.*
20. Skinflint—A hard, stingy person; a miser.

Every word in English has a characteristic sound. It is important to maintain the 'tone' (resonant, pungent, amusing, etc.) to preserve the true nature of the word. Changing the tone can often make the word look different and it may end in an error. So care has to taken to get the correct meaning.

Given below are some interesting snippets on words and their related subjects.

1. We have often seen the symbol '&' being used to denote 'and', known as an Ampersand.
2. We have often heard of the expression 'French leave'. What would a person be doing if he is on a French leave? It means he has left the workplace without permission.
3. How did the word 'hat trick' originate? In the past, a cricketer who took three wickets in three successive balls was entitled to a new hat at the expense of the club. Thus the phrase.
4. According to one version whose last words were "Eloi Eloi Lama Sabacthani" which means "My God, my God, why hast thou forsaken me?" Jesus Christ.

5. What do the words 'uxorious', 'uxoricide' and 'univocalis' mean?

   Uxorious—*The Shorter Oxford* (1993 ed.) defines uxorious as 'greatly or excessively fond of one's wife, doting'.

   Uxoricide—Killing one's wife, a crime of passion which is the subject of Shakespeare's *Othello*.

   Univocalis—Poems or prose in which only one vowel is used throughout. (Here we must learn what a Lipogram is: Lipograms are works in which all the vowels, barring one are used.)

6. 'Moped' is the short term for *motorised pedalling*.
   a. 'Pop music' is *popular music* shortened.
   b. 'Bus' is the short term for *omnibus* that means for everybody.
   c. 'Fortnight' comes from *fourteen nights* (2 weeks).
   d. 'Drawing' room was actually a *withdrawing room* where people withdrew after dinner. Later the prefix 'with' was dropped.
   e. 'Journal' is a diary that tells about *journey* for a day during each day's business.
   f. 'Queue' comes from *queen's quest*. Long back a long row of people was waiting to see the queen. Someone made the comment, *queen's quest*.

   'Tips' comes from the expression 'to ensure prompt service' in older days to get prompt service from servants in an inn. Travellers used to drop coins in a box on which was written ' To ensure prompt service'. This gave rise to the custom of tips.

When we learn the origin of words we always learn to use them better; we also become aware of the correct context to use term.

7. English has a vocabulary of two million words; French by comparison has only 60,000 words.
8. What do the terms 'logophilia' and 'logomania' mean? Both the terms mean 'Love of words'.
9. 'Monde green' is a cockeyed term or phrase resulting from mishearing the proper term (a cousin, if you like) of

a malapropism. Monde greens are mostly committed by kids learning the language but adults are not immune. For example, Hemlock remover for the Heimlich Manoeuvre.

10. The longest word listed in a dictionary is usually a disease. It is Pneumonoultramicroscopic Silico volcanoconiosis. It is a word containing 45 letters.

11. 'Love all the tennis'. Love comes from the French *Loeuf* which means an egg. The egg has been for a long time symbolised 'zero'. So when the empire says 'love all' he means the score is zero-zero. No one has scored a point yet. This is one of the explanation. Some others have suggested that 'love' comes from the phrase "for the love" of the game. In the old days people played because they enjoyed the game (they didn't play for money as today).

'love all' in tennis means the score is zero-zero.

12. Blinkers – The leather patches that are put around the eyes of a horse are called blinkers. When these patches are fixed beside the horse's eyes the animal is forced to look straight ahead. It cannot see what is happening at the sides. When you say that an individual wears blinkers it means he has a limited view of something. He does not completely understand or know all aspects of the situation.

13. What is a person doing if he is tickling the 'ivories'?
He is playing the piano.

a. What is 'Dutch courage'?
Displaying courage after consuming intoxicating drinks.

Tickling the ivories means playing the piano.

b. What is a 'catch 22' situation?
It is a no-win situation or dilemma arising out of conflicting condition. It was taken from Joseph Heller's novel Catch 22.

c. If you 'bowdlerise' a book, what are you doing?
You omit certain unsuitable words.
What is a 'tongue in cheek remark'? The real important phrase is to keep a civil tongue in your cheek which gets abbreviated to 'tongue in cheek remark'. The implication is a snide, uncivil remark which cannot be understood at the first instance unless a person has his wits around him.

26

QUEER PHRASES

Recently a magazine carried an article titled 'Some New phrases'. Certain phrases appeared comical. Given below are the various new phrases in this section. The reader can use his/her discretion regarding the use (or useless) nature of them.

1. Shnovel—A self-book disguised as a novel.
2. Single digit midget—A company with a stock price below ten dollars.
3. Slackademic—A perpetual student who prefers the safety and comfort of academic life over the trials and tribulations of the real world.
4. Smoking letter—A memo, a letter or e-mail message that contains irrefutable evidence of a crime.
5. Space invader—Someone who violates the personal space of other people by standing too close during conversations.
6. Surgiholic – A person who seeks plastic surgery from head to toe and is never satisfied (this word reminds us of pop star Michael Jackson).
7. Schmooseoisie—The ever expanding class of people who make their living by talking either on talk radio or on TV talk shows.
8. Screenager—A young person who has grown up with and is therefore entirely comfortable with a world of screens, TV, computers.
9. Sheeple—People who are meek, easily persuaded and tend to follow the crowd (sheep+people).
10. Yettie—A young person who owns a technology outfit.

SURGIHOLIC ?

The word "surgiholic" suits the Pop singer MIchael **Jackson** very perfectly. He has this obsession of seeking plastic surgery for his various parts of the body (especially nose (nose job ?)) and is never satisfied. We seem to be reading about his plastic surgeries all the time in news papers.

The evolution of such new words and phrases are mostly influenced by various personalities / celebrities referred to as 'glitterretti'. As we all know 'fact is stranger than fiction' - & hence these words often remain a understatement. (to what they / whom they mean)

11. Dadrock—Music performed by aging rock stars.
12. Dead cat bounce—A temporary recovery from a major drop in a stock's price.
13. Dead tree edition—The paper version of an online magazine or journal.
14. Dellionaire—A rich person whose wealth is based on owning stock in Dell Computer Corporation.
15. Desk fast—A breakfast eaten at your desk.
16. Diet cop—A person hired to monitor a celebrity's weight loss programme.
17. Dins—Double income, no sex – a new acronym that sociologists are using to describe today's stressed out couples.
18. Dittography—The accidental repetition of one or more letters when writing or typing a word.
19. Ditto heads—People who mindlessly agree on one idea because it fits in their ideology or because they are followers of the person who put forth the idea.
20. Dread merchant—A person who makes a living by predicting disasters and worst case scenarios.
21. Adhocracy—An organisation with little or no structure, the opposite of bureaucracy.

22. Affluenza—An extreme form of materialism in which consumer over work accumulates high levels of debt in order to purchase more goods.
23. Armcandy—An extremely beautiful person who accompanies a member of the opposite sex to a party or event but is not romantically involved with that person.
24. Technoplegic—A person who feels paralysed mentally when faced with technology.

Will these words get recognition and licence in English grammar? Will these words enter a dictionary or a thesaurus? Only time will tell, but a question that springs in our mind after going through these words is—should one discuss the common errors in English or an English which is in the process of becoming an error in itself?

27

NOUNS AND THEIR VARIOUS FORMS

Errors in using nouns can be in the following ways.

1. Errors in agreement with verbs.
2. Errors in the use of plurals.
3. Errors in case.

Errors in agreement with verbs can be avoided by determining the noun or pronoun which is the true subject of the verb and then determining whether it is singular or plural. One must keep in mind that a verb agrees with its subject in number and in person. If the subject (noun or the pronoun) is first person singular, the verb must also be first person singular.

Example: Gita is the principal. I am the vice-principal.

In the following sentences we can see the errors that arise when the subject of the verb is not determined. One must determine the real subject to avoid errors.

Wrong

1. A box of candy *are* on the table.
2. Her thoughtlessness and indecency *annoys* me.
3. The *memoranda* is important (memoranda is plural).
4. A trio of girl *were* schedule to dance (wrong because the subject of the verb is the singular noun "trio").

Right

1. A box of candies *is* on the table.
2. Her thoughtlessness and indecency *annoy* me.
3. The memoranda *are* important.
4. A trio of girls *was* scheduled to dance.

Writers and speakers must be especially careful of sentences in which parenthetical elements appear between the subject and the verb because these elements often mislead the writer or the speaker into using a plural verb. For example, in the sentence, *Sita as well as Radha is responsible for this act,* the verb "is" (a singular form) is used because its subject is Sita, which is singular. The phrase "as well as Radha" is a parenthetical element and consequently has no bearing on the subject.

Wrong: Mr. Gopal together with some friends and neighbours are planning a celebration.

Right: Mr. Gopal together with some friends and neighbours is planning a celebration.

Next let us consider the collective nouns.

A collective noun, as the name implies, is a noun that represents a collection. It is a noun that stands for two or more persons, objects or ideas. Generally collective nouns are regarded as being singular, and consequently they require singular verbs.

The Jury are arguing among themselves.

Example: The militia is quartered in its barracles.

Sometimes however they convey a plural idea, and in these instances they require a plural verb.

Example: The militia are discussing the bottle among themselves.

Given below are some examples of common errors in agreement that arise with the use of collective nouns as subject of verbs.

Example: The jury is arguing among itself (wrong because the jury is not arguing collectively). Rather its members are arguing among themselves.

Right: The Jury *are* arguing among themselves.
Potato chips *are* the first item on the menu.
Right: Potato chips *is* the first item on the menu.

Frequently there are situations wherein two or more persons, object or ideas which are otherwise singular combine to make a collective thought.

Example: Arun and Kumar at the same bridge table is unthinkable.

The noun Arun and Kumar constitute a collective thought. Hence the singular verb 'is' rather than the plural verb 'are' is used. Collective idea requires a singular verb.

Wrong: Alexander and Parker are a law firm.
Right: Alexander and Parker is a law firm.
Wrong: Bread and fruit are my favourite breakfast.
Right: Bread and fruit is my favourite breakfast.

Next, let us consider the subjects joined by the conjunction 'or'. When two nouns or pronouns acting as the subject of a verb are joined by the conjunction 'or' the second named noun or pronoun governs the choice of the verb.

Example: Arun or I am to clean the place.
Gopal or he is to complete the lesson.
They or we are to occupy the first table.

The conjunction 'or' really makes two sentences and hence this rule is followed. The first sentences above for instance actually states.

Arun is to clean the place or I am to clean the place.

Cetain similar examples include:

Wrong: Vidya or I *are* to lead the procession.
Right: Vidya or I *am* to lead the procession.
Wrong: Arun or he *are* to call the roll.
Right: Arun or he *is* to call the roll.
Wrong: They or he *are* certain to be included.
Right: They or he *is* certain to be included.
Wrong: Prakash or I *are* to lead the march.
Right: Prakash or I *is* to lead the march.

A common error made by children and carried into adult life is the double subject. Below are examples with the corrected form.

Wrong: Gita's sister *she* took the car home.
Right: Gita's sister took the car home.
Wrong: Gopal and I *we* took the short cut to school.
Right: Gopal and I took the short cut to school.

Sometimes it is thought that insertion of a comma between the subject and the double subject justifies the use of the double subject as a correct usage, but this concept is wrong. For example, the sentences below are incorrect, notwithstanding the use of the comma.

Wrong: The players, they liked the concept.
Right: The players liked the concept.
Wrong: The stereotype department, it makes the mat.
Right: The stereotype department makes the mat.

So far we have discussed about determining the real subject, parenthetical elements between subject and verb, collective nouns, collective ideas, subject joined by the conjunction 'or' and double subject.

Let us examine *there is* and *there are*. One must first know that any sentence beginning with either of these expression is *inverted* and therefore one should cast the sentences into its *natural* rather than its inverted order. Natural order refers to placing the subject before the verb. The following example will help you understand this concept.

There are two books on the shelf (Inverted).

Two books are there on the shelf (Natural).

When a sentence of this type is placed in its natural order the recognition of subject becomes very easy. Deciding whether the verb is to be singular or plural also becomes easy.

Wrong: There *are* a group ready to enter the theatre now (wrong because the subject is the noun group).
Right: There *is* a group ready to enter the room now.
Wrong: Here *comes* my sister and her friend.
Right: Here *come* my sister and her friend.

There is a lot of doubt regarding correlative conjunctions and subject. A correlative conjunction is one which works in correlation with another conjunction. Examples are 'either..or'; 'neither nor'; 'as...as'; 'not so as'. When nouns or pronouns acting as subject are used with correlative conjunctions, the choice of the verb is determined by the second noun or pronoun.

Example: Either Arun or Gopal is coming.
Neither Vidya nor I am leaving.

In the sentences above the verb agrees with the second noun or pronoun.

Wrong: Neither Ram nor Shyaam are responsible (wrong because the verb must agree with the singular noun "Shyaam").
Right: Neither Ram nor Shyaam is responsible.
Wrong: Either Wilson or Eugene are represented.
Right: Either Wilson or Eugene is represented.

Let us now discuss about nouns that are always plural. While many of these nouns are commonly misused as singulars by giving them singular verbs, they are plural. Therefore they require plural verbs.

clothes	billiards	entrails	pincers
leavings	ashes	oats	remains
goods	annals	nuptials	riches
dregs		pants	scissors
links	eaves	proceeds	shears
suds	thongs	skippers	thanks
trousers	vitals	spectacles	tongs
tweezers	wages		

Wrong: My scissors *is* very sharp.
Right: My scissors *are* very sharp.
Wrong: Her clothes *is* certainly costly.
Right: Her clothes *are* certainly costly.

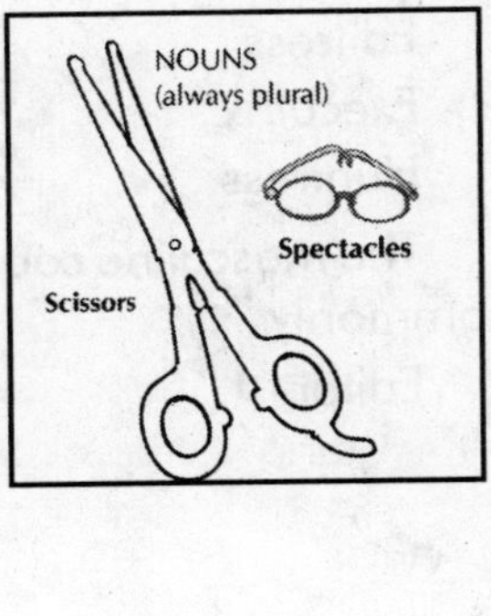

There are nouns that are always

singular. The nouns that are always plural and nouns which may be either. Some plural nouns are considered singular in meaning and therefore require singular verbs.

athletics	dynamics	magnetics	phonics	statistics
alms	ethics	mathematics	physics	tactics
acoustics	economics	mumps	poetics	United States
bellows	hydraulics	news	rickets	whereabouts
comics	linguistics	optics	statics	politics

Some of the above words can be plural on rather unusual occasions.

Example: The acoustics of the two buildings are sharply different (right because acoustics is basically plural).

On some occasions singular forms replace plural forms when the noun becomes an objective. In spite of the singular form being used, the word remains plural as far as the meaning is considered. See the following examples.

1. Mrs. Kapoor wants a three-room home.
2. We walked two miles. It was therefore a two-mile walk.
3. Mr. Sharma is building a three-car garage.

In all the above examples singular forms are used as plurals in the right way. One should be careful in such usages.

Let us now examine the feminine and masculine forms. The recent trend is to use masculine forms for both masculine and feminine form of nouns.

Some feminine forms of nouns are rarely used, like the following:

Editress　　Poetess
Executrix　　Benefactress
Huntress

The masculine counterparts of the above nouns are used more commonly.

Editor

Executor Poet
Hunter Benefactor

Example: Edna St. Vincent Millay, an American poetess, wrote many fine sonnets.

The current form is to use 'poet' instead of 'poetess'.

She is a great poet
(much used)

Feminine noun forms like administratrix, directress, inheritrix have all been dropped; their masculine counter parts have become the accepted forms of usage.

Chairperson, Ms have all now come into use to end a controversy over masculine and feminine genders 'Ms' makes irrelevant a woman marital status and chairperson ends the controversy over chairman and chairlady. 'Gentle persons' to be used in the place of gentlemen has not gained much popularity. Gender bias can be avoided by using such new forms which seem more acceptable.

Errors in the Use of Pronouns

Errors in the use of pronouns can be classified under four headings:

1. Errors in agreement with verbs.
2. Errors arising with the use of antecedent.
3. Errors in case.
4. Miscellaneous errors.

Certain basic rules for agreement of subject and verb which were discussed above must be considered here also. The rules apply to pronouns also. In this section we will be dealing with errors in agreement with verbs that pertain to pronouns exclusively. We will be also discussing errors arising with the use of antecedents and various miscellaneous errors.

One must always remember that a verb must agree with its subject in number and in person. Pronouns are difficult to handle as some of them are always singular and some are always plural, and some may be either plural or singular.

Wrong: Everybody *accept their* responsibilities.

Right: Everybody *accepts his* responsibilities.

Wrong: Everyone *were* singing from *their* books as they entered the room. (Wrong because the verb and the pronouns substituted for 'everyone' do not agree with the singular pronoun 'everyone').

Right: Everyone *was* singing from *his* books as he entered the room.

Wrong: Nobody in that group *have their* reports up to date as they should have.

Right: Nobody in that group *has his* reports up to date as he should have.

Let us now see 'either' and 'neither'. These can be correlative conjunction, adjectives, pronouns. See the following examples:

1. Either Ramu or am I to speak next (Correlative conjunction).
2. Either player may be used at half back (Adjective).
3. Neither is a very reliable substitute (Pronoun). When 'either' or 'neither' is used as a pronoun, it is always singular.
4. Either of the boys are acceptable to do the errands (wrong because the verb should be singular to agree with the subject either).
5. Either of the boys is acceptable to do the errands.

Most of people have doubt on the use of *'it'* as a pronoun. When the pronoun 'it' is used indefinitely, it is singular, even though the noun in the predicate may be plural. (The indefinite 'it' is frequently termed as an "expletive".)

Wrong: It are the freshman who feel this regulation most keenly (wrong because the indefinite "it" requires a singular verb).

Right: It is the freshman who feels this regulation most keenly.

When the words 'both', 'few', 'many', 'several' are used as pronouns, they are always plural and therefore require plural verbs.

Wrong: Both the mice is underfed.
Right: Both the mice are underfed.
Wrong: Of all the cartons few is left.
Right: Of all the cartons few are left.

The words 'all', 'any', 'none', 'some' used as pronouns may be singular or plural according to their meaning.

Right: All I have left is a few packets ('All' represents in essence a collective idea).
Right: All the club are planning to attend ('All' represents a plural number of members).
Right: Is any of the chocolate left?
Right: Are any of the girls here?
Right: None of the cards are here.

The pronoun 'one' should be used in the general sense of 'anyone' or 'everyone'. The pronoun 'you' should be used only when addressing a specific person or persons, i.e., second person use.

Wrong: If *you* live in Chicago one day and in Las Vegas you are certain to feel the change in temperature (wrong because this fact is true of anyone having this experience).
Right: If *one* lives in Chicago one day and in Las Vegas the next one is certain to feel the change in temperature.

In days gone by, grammarians insisted on an extensive and precise pattern of rules to govern the use of 'he', 'she', 'his', 'her' but now the rules have been relaxed. The pronouns *he* and *his* are to be used in situations involving only the male sex or in situations involving both the male and the female sexes.

Every student must take his book with him to class (It can refer to male only/or to males and females).

In situations involving the female sex alone the practice is now to use female pronouns.

Example: Every student must sign her name on her report card.

When a relative pronoun is acting as the subject of a verb, one must be careful to recognise its antecedent (the noun or pronoun to which it refers), because the number and the person of the antecedent determines the number and the person of the verb.

Example: It is I who am the winner ("who" is first person singular because its antecedent "I" is first person singular therefore the verb "am" must agree with "who").

Wrong: John is one of the boys who is on time (wrong because in this sentence the antecedent of 'who' is 'boys'. Note that the word 'the' does not appear in this sentence).

Right: John is one of the boys who are on time.

A pronoun must agree with its antecedent in number, gender and person (the term antecedent means the noun or the pronoun to which a later pronoun refers).

Wrong: It is I who is next (wrong because the antecedent of 'who' is 'I').

Right: It is I who am next.

Occasionally a pronoun that normally refers to an antecedent may be used without an antecedent. In such cases the antecedent is implied.

Right: As the crowd began to assemble in the conference room the president began to scan *their* faces (here the antecedent of 'their' is not the 'crowd' but it can be 'members', 'ministers' or some similar term that is implied).

One often has doubt in the use of "its" and "it's" a short form for it is.

Wrong: The dog has it's bone.
Right: The dog has its bone.
Wrong: Its a long way home.
Right: It's a long way home. (It is a long way home.)

The practice of using the relative pronouns 'that' and 'this' without a concrete antecedent has a tendency to make the sentence vague.

Wrong: Mr. Thomas was always interrupting his sister. That annoyed her very much.

Right: Mr. Thomas was always interrupting his sister. His interruptions annoyed her very much.

Wrong: Mr. Peter always arrives on time and he works steadily until the final whistle. This is very important in the business world.

Right: Mr. Peter always arrives on time and he works steadily until the final whistle. *Punctuality* and *industry* are very important in the business world.

The pronoun 'they' must not be used carelessly in an indefinite sense – especially when it is not needed. When a pronoun is used without a definite antecedent, it may result in vague reference.

Wrong: Our teacher told us that in France they eat horse meat.

Right: Our teacher told us that the French eat horse meat.

It is considered that use of the word 'theirselves', is not correct; the correct form is themselves.

Wrong: They are hurting theirselves by their anger.

Right: They are hurting themselves by their anger.

Now we shall briefly discuss the use of 'them', 'what', 'which', 'who', 'whose' and 'whom'.

The pronoun 'them' may never be used as a demonstrative adjective.

Wrong: He put them cartons on the shelf.

Right: He put those cartons on the shelf.

'What' is now accepted as an all purpose pronoun. Formal English however:

1. does not permit 'what' to have an antecedent;
2. does not allow the substitution of 'what' for 'that which'.

Wrong: This is the case what I want (wrong because 'what' has an antecedent 'case').

Right: This is the case that I want.

The relative pronoun 'which' must not be used in a manner that creates doubt about its antecedent.

Right: We shall drive if the road are clear as I think they are.

Wrong: We shall drive if the road are clear which I think they are.

'Who' is termed a relative pronoun, an interrogative pronoun and a personal pronoun according to its function in a given instance. 'Who' should be used only to refer to people. It should be used as a nominative case pronoun only.

Wrong: Who did you choose yesterday? (wrong because the pronoun 'who' is being used as the object of the verb 'choose').

Wrong: The lion who stands in the first cage is really large (here 'who' is not being used to refer people hence wrong).

The right statements are:

Right: Whom did you choose yesterday?

Right: The lion that stands in the first cage is really large.

The pronoun 'whose' is now being used to refer both an inanimate object as well as a person. Previously it was not permitted to use 'whose' in instances where its antecedent was an inanimate object. The following examples explain the use of 'whose'.

Example: It was a school whose excellence was beyond question

Example: This is a magazine whose circulation has risen sharply.

'Whom' like 'who' is a relative, an interrogative and a personal pronoun. The following examples show the correct use of 'whom'.

1. Whom did the teacher give the project work?
2. Whom did you see last night in Mumbai?
3. Whom should I give the parcel to now?
4. Whom do you want to help you?
5. Whom should I take with me to dinner?

Errors in Case

Many errors in usage stem from a lack of knowledge of case. Case means the relationship of a noun/pronoun to another word in the sentence. If a noun or pronoun serve as the subject of a verb, is said to be in the nominative case. If on the other hand it serves as the object of a verb it is said to be in the objective case.

Every noun and pronoun is in one of the three cases – nomination, objective, possessive. The function determines the case of a noun or pronoun, and recognition of the function of the noun or pronoun constitutes the rules for the case.

To determine the function of noun or pronouns one must know how to divide the sentences into elements. The term 'element' means a natural grouping of words. This constitutes the verb and every word related to it.

Consider the following sentence.

It is I who am to drive for you.

The elements are:

'It is I'.

'who am to drive'.

'for you'.

Sometimes the grouping of elements may seem not so natural.

Whom do you want, may I ask, for this role?

The elements in this sentence are:

"you do want whom"

"I may ask"

"for this role"

How does one establish the case of a noun or a pronoun. First one should confirm that a given word is a noun or pronoun. Then one must break up the sentence into elements; determine the function of the noun/pronoun in the element and hence determine its case.

Nouns do not change their form except in the possessive case. Pronoun can present difficulties. One should know the pronominal forms for the three cases (nominative, objective, possessive). The following table gives the pronouns for the three cases.

Nominative Case	*Objective Case*	*Possessive Case*
I	Me	My
You	You	Your
She	Her	Her
He	Him	His
It	It	Its
We	Us	Our
They	Them	Their
Who	Whom	Whose

The subject of a verb is always in the nominative case. If a pronoun is to be used as the subject of a verb, it must be nominative case pronoun (as in the above table). The following sentence illustrates the noun and the pronoun used as subject of a verb.

Wrong: Gita and me are the first in line.
Right: Gita and I are the first in line.
Wrong: Arun and her were in the front row.
Right: Arun and she were in the front row.

Here we must know what a predicate nominative is. A predicate nominative is a noun or a pronoun which has three features: it is located in the predicate (the part of the sentence from the verb onwards); it usually follows a form of the verb "to be" (i.e., 'am', 'is', 'was', 'were', 'be', 'been'); it always renames the subject. The predict nominative is also called as subjective complement and predictive noun. If a person is serving as a predicative nominative it must be a nominative case pronoun (as in the table). The following sentences show predicate nominatives:

Wrong: The leader may be him, but I don't think so.
Right: The leader may be he, but I don't think so.
Wrong: If I were him, I should not accept the gift.
Right: If I were he, I should not accept the gift.

The object of a verb is always in the objective case. Hence, the pronoun used as the object of a verb must be objective case pronouns. The following examples illustrate the object of a verb.

Wrong: The coach put Arun and I on the first team.
Right: The coach put Arun and me on the first team.
Wrong: We chose Gopal and she for the committee.
Right: We chose Gopal and her for the committee.

Nouns and pronouns serving as the object of a preposition are in the objective case. In such a case the pronouns must be objective case pronouns.

Wrong: The answer looked wrong to Kavita and he.
Right: The answer looked wrong to Kavita and him.
Wrong: Gita demanded assistance for Sita and she.
Right: Gita demanded assistance for Sita and her.

The indirect object of the verb is always in the objective case. Hence only objective case pronouns may be used to serve as indirect object of verbs (the indirect object of a verb is always the object of the preposition "to" or the proposition "for").

Wrong: Please read for Ganesh and I that story.
Right: Please read for Ganesh and me that story.
Wrong: The coach gave they and we a lecture.
Right: The coach gave them and us a lecture.

The subject of the infinitive is always in the objective case. So when pronouns are used as the subject of infinitives, they must be objective case pronouns.

Wrong: That was John who the captain asked to help the corporal.
Right: That was John whom the captain asked to help the corporal.
Wrong: The teacher told he and I to study maths.
Right: The teacher told him and me to study maths.

We must know that the word 'but' has the meaning of 'except'. Under such a meaning it becomes a preposition. Therefore its object (noun or pronoun) falls in the objective case.

Example: Everyone was there but me (pronoun is in the objective case as it is the object of the preposition 'but').

Errors can occur in such cases with 'but' as preposition where there is a compound (two or more) object. See the following examples.

Wrong: They did not object to anyone but Gopal and he.
Right: They did not object to anyone but Gopal and him.
Wrong: No Juniors but she and he really wanted the rule.
Right: No Juniors but her and him really wanted the rule.

Let us now turn to *Gerunds*. A gerund is the 'ing' form of a verb used as noun. For example, walking, running, swimming, singing, dancing. If the gerund is to be modified by a noun or a pronoun (it becomes an adjective). The noun or the pronoun must be in the possessive case if it stands for a person. See the following examples:

Mother objected to Mary dancing.
Mother objected to Mary's dancing.

Wrong: Mother objected to Mary dancing.
Right: Mother objected to Mary's dancing.
Wrong: Mr. Sharma disliked me asking so many questions.
Right: Mr. Sharma disliked my asking so many questions.

There is often a lot of confusion between a gerund and a present participle. One must remember that the case of the accompanying noun or pronoun is different in each instance. The following discussion tries to delineate the various differences between gerunds and present participles. You understand these differences clearly and avoid errors associated with them.

	Gerund	**Present Participle**
1.	'ing' form of verb used as a noun	'ing' form of verb used as an adjective; of a present participle. Example:

	1. The singing waiter entered the room ('singing' modifies the noun 'waiter'). 2. Singing merrily, he entered the room ('singing' modifies the pronoun 'he').
2. If the gerund is used the accompanying noun or pronoun must be in the possessive case	If a present participle is used the accompanying noun or pronoun is in either the nominative or objective case, according to its function (participle thus modifies the noun or pronoun).

The difficulty arises in using the gerund and the participle of certain verbs because either one may often be used logically. The speaker or writer must be careful as he may create a meaning he does not want. See the following sentences which use the gerund and the participle.

1. We pictured *him* shouting at the audience (shouting is a participle).

   We pictured *his* shouting at the audience (shouting is a gerund).
2. Mother saw him eating an orange (eating is a participle. Therefore, mother saw him as a person).

   Mother saw his eating an orange (eating is a gerund. Therefore, mother saw the act).

Before we conclude this discussion two points need a brief mention.

1. The use of possessive forms with inanimate object. Objects without life should be avoided if possible.

Wrong: The tree's upper branches need pruning.
Right: The upper branches of the tree need pruning.

There are some instances (a day's work, a year's growth) where the possessive with inanimate object has become very firmly established. That it cannot be avoided.

2. The other point is about the reflexive pronouns. A reflexive pronoun (myself, yourself, himself, etc.) may not be substituted for a nominative or an objective case pronoun in formal English.

Wrong: She chose Arun and myself for the task.
Right: She chose Arun and me for the task.

When the subject of the verb is also the receiver of the action, the action is reflected. Hence to reflect action reflexive pronouns are used.

Right: Gopal gives himself credit for the promotion.
Right: Varun cut himself while shaving.

Reflexive pronouns are used for emphasis and in certain idiomatic expressions.

Right: Gita did the work herself (emphasis).
Right: I myself do not care (idiomatic; this sentence really says, I do not care how this situation affects me, but I am concerned about others).

28

SOME DOUBTS ABOUT ENGLISH USAGE

1. In English language what is 'syncope'?

   Omitting letters in the middle of a word is called a syncope.

2. What is the origin of the term 'white elephant'? How to use it?

   It is said that if ever the King of Siam wanted to ruin his courtiers he would present them with a white elephant. The courtries could not return the present and at the same time could not afford to keep the elephant.

   Hence the term.

WHITE ELEPHANT

White elephant refers to a useless possession, e.g., a big house which is proving difficult to maintain.

It is used to mean or denote anything which is huge / grand and difficult to maintain.

Example: My aunt considers her old mansion a white elephant as she cannot maintain it.

3. What is the difference between 'rain' and 'rainfall'?

   'Rain' is a noun. It refers to atmospheric moisture falling as drops: 'shower of things'. 'Hail, refers to pellets of frozen rain falling in a shower'; shower of blows; question. This is the meaning of hail as a noun; as a verb it means to greet or acclaim. 'Rainfall' refers to total mount of rain falling in a given time.

Examples

a. There was a heavy rainfall recorded in Red Hills today.
b. Just as I got out of the house it began to rain.
c. The rainfall his year in Tamil Nadu is good.
d. We have good rain. (noun)
e. It rained well. (verb)

   Certain associated words are:

   Drizzling – rain in very fine drops.

   Shower – moderate rain (this can mean a mild to moderate rain).

   Downpour – heavy rain.

4. What is the meaning of the term 'talking shop'? Talking about business matters outside work is called 'talking' shop. It is probably called so because talking factory or talking office would sound even sillier. Talking shop means discussing office matters with colleagues when not at work.
5. What does cutting the 'Gordian knot' mean? Solving a difficult problem in an unusual manner.
6. Who is a 'quisling' and how did the word originate? He is a traitor to his country. The term has come into usage after Quisling, a Norwegian, who collaborated with Germany against his motherland.
7. Is it possible to make a sentence with all the twenty-six letters of the English alphabet?

   Yes, the following sentence has all the 26 letters PACK MY NAVY BOX WITH DOZEN JUGS OF LIQUOR.

8. How did the term 'flea markets' originate? Markets selling second-hand goods become popular in France in the early 1900s. They were known as *Marches aux puces* (flea markets) because old items were thought to be full of fleas!

9. What is this word 'Circa' associated with time mean? 'Circa' is a formal word which is used before a year to indicate that something happened around that time but not exactly in that particular year. In other words, it informs you of the approximate year when something happened. *Examples*: They found manuscripts dating from circa 500.
The fort was built in circa 1463.
Some scholars claim that he was born in circa 400 BC.

10. What is the origin of the expression 'to bark up the wrong tree'? This expression comes from the sport of raccoon hunting. A raccoon is a small furry animal found mostly in America. These animals, being nocturnal, are hunted in the night time. In order to catch them hunters make use of dogs. The dog's job is to chase these animals and drive them up a tree. Once a raccoon is driven up a tree the dogs stand under the tree and keep barking. This is their way of telling their masters that there is an animal hiding in the tree. Sometimes of course the dogs pick the wrong tree to bark at – one in which there is no raccoon. So when you say that someone is barking up the wrong tree it means he has made the wrong choice. He will not succeed in doing what he wants to because he is following the wrong course of action.

— To bark up the wrong tree

Examples

a. If you think you are going to get Lakshmi's job by being nice to the chairman, you are barking up the wrong tree.

b. We all believed that it was Rahul who killed the woman but we were all barking up the wrong tree.

11. What does the term 'hen party' mean? It is a party to which only ladies are invited. The men are strictly kept out. Before a wedding the bride and her friend (only female friends) usually get together and have a good time. This would be called a 'hen party'. A 'stag party' is one to which only men are invited.

12. What is the origin of the idiom 'skeleton in the cupboard'? This idiom was popularised by the English novelist William Thackeray. The idiom in itself is based on an earlier legend of a king trying to find someone who had no worries in the world. The story goes that a king wanted to find someone in his kingdom who was very happy, someone who did not have any problems. After a lot of searching they found a lady. His ministers (who were sent to find such a person) were happy that she fit the description of a perfect happy person. When she was informed that she had been chosen as the one person in the entire kingdom who did not have any problems, she took the men upstairs and opened a cupboard. Inside there was a skeleton. She informed the men that the skeleton was that of her lover's. He had been killed by her husband in duel. "I try to keep my trouble to myself but every night my husband compels me to see that skeleton." The idiom means a past happening which is kept as a secret. There are other explanations as to how the idiom originated too. This idiom is used to denote a past happening (something bad, horrible) which is kept as a secret unknown to everybody.

Examples

a. I thought Gopi was a happy man but his past seems to have many skeletons in the cupboard.

b. Mrs. Sharada is a very inquisitive person and wants to dig skeleton in the cupboard of her friend.

13. What is the origin of the phrases 'Eleventh hour', and how should it be used? 'Eleventh hour' is so called from a parable of vineyard where labourers hired at the eleventh hour or the latest possible time are paid the same wages as those hired early in the day. It is used to mean the last, latest moment.

    Examples

    a. He prepared for the exams at the eleventh hour.
    b. She reached the interview spot at the eleventh hour.
    c. We got the tickets for the movie at the eleventh hour.

14. How should one use the phrase 'at the drop of a hat'? The phrase means to respond immediately on a signal without delay. It originated from the American frontier practice of dropping a hat as a signal for a fight to begin, usually the only formality observed. Races are sometimes started by the downward sweep of a hat. One should use this phrase to show somebody's eagerness to obey or respond immediately to somebody's instruction that too a mild one.

    Example: Gita begins to sing at the drop of a hat.

    Arun start showing his paintings at the drop of a hat.

15. The term 'cloud nine' means a state of extreme happiness. According to Christian mythology heaven has been divided

into cloud one, two, three and so on. Cloud nine is the one where all the wishes of a person are granted. That is why whenever we are elated we exclaim that we are on cloud nine. Cloud nine should be used only to express an extreme state of elation.

Example: Varun is on cloud nine since he got the US visa.

Lakshmi is on cloud nine since her medical admission.

16. What do the terms 'lotus eater', 'southpaw', 'man Friday' mean? Lotus eater is one who is forgetful and careless about responsibilities, living only for pleasure. The original lotus eaters or *loto phagi* were a people whom Odysseus and his men encountered in Homer's *Odyssey*. They lived on lotus which they offered to travellers. Those who ate it forgot home, friends, responsibilities and wanted only to lie in the sun and eat the lotus forever.

    Hence, a lotus eater is used to denote a person who is careless, carefree and not serious about responsibilities.
    Examples

    a. Prakash sleeps the whole day, parties the whole night—a jolly good lotus eater he is.
    b. Arun drinks, smokes, goes to pubs to party with girl friends isn't he a perfect lotus eater !

    A left hander is called southpaw, after the left-handed boxer 'Tobias Southpaw' whose 'punishing left' put his opponents right out for the count. Also because most base-ball fields are laid out with the homeplate towards the west and left hand towards south. Therefore, a left-hander is called a southpaw.

    Example: Cricketer Sourav Ganguly is a southpaw.

Southpaw
A left hander

The term 'man Friday' originates from a classic story written by Daniel Defoe of *Robinson Crusoe* fame who was marooned on a lone island for sixteen years. Friday was a wild slave whom he had rescued on Friday and who became his loyal attandent, slave, cook and bodyguard.

This term is used to denote somebody who has the above attributes, who is very helpful, loyal; and does all the work, however hard it may be.

Example: 'Here comes Ravi, our man Friday!' exclaimed his friends.

17. What is the origin of the phrase 'I don't give a damn'? This phrase has a diluted origin. One identifies the damn with an Indian coin of trivial value. Another suggestions is that the damn was a piece of clay used by a tinker to stop a hole in a kettle or pot while he repaired it from outside. The damn was then discarded. This damn is also known as cuss, hence the low value set on "a tinker's cuss". Against the theory of the Hindi origin is the fact that the word would be heard by English ears as 'dawn'. Oliver Goldsmith did not care three damns and the Duke of Wellington (who made his name in India) 'did not care a two-penny damn'. The debate continues. 'My dear I don't give a damn' is a statement made by Rhett Butler to Scarlet O'Hara in Margaret Mitchell's novel *Gone with the Wind*. Scarlet asks Rhett what she would do if Rhett parts from her. Rhett hesitates, shrugs and then, after a small hesitation, says, 'My dear, I don't give a damn!' The phrase appears at the end of the movie when Rhett leaves Scarlet high and dry to go his own way. This phrase is used to denote the expression 'I don't care' or 'It will not be affecting me the least'. This expression is very popular among youngsters who utter it very often.

Example: Even if my dad scolds me I give a damn. I give a damn as to what the society thinks about me.

18. To 'eat humble pie' means to apologise humbly or to ask forgiveness under humiliating circumstances. The expression originated presumably during the pre-decimalisation days.

Examples

a. Neeta had to eat humble pie after being caught eavesdropping.

b. The police had to eat humble pie knowing that they had arrested the wrong person for the robbery case.

29

VERBS AND THEIR VARIOUS FORMS

The various errors in the use of verbs are:

1. Errors in agreement with subject.
2. Errors in tense and voice.
3. Errors in splitting forms and in mood.

The term 'tense' means time. One should use proper tense in one's speech and writing to establish a proper time relationship. There are three basic or primary tenses in English: The past, the present and the future.

There are three secondary tenses: past perfect, present perfect, future perfect.

There are also several variations on each of these three primary and three secondary tenses. The past tense is used to denote the past time. The present tense is used to denote that which pertains to the present time. The future tense is used to denote that which will happen at to a future time.

Past Tense

I spoke.	We spoke.
He spoke.	They spoke.
You spoke.	You spoke.

Present Tense

I speak.	We speak.
He speaks.	They speak.
You speak.	She speaks.

Future Tense

I shall speak.	We shall speak.
He will speak.	They will speak.
You will speak.	She will speak.

The past perfect tense denotes that which occurred before a specific moment in the past.

When you entered (the specific moment in the past), I had completed my work (the action before the specific moment in the past).

The conjugation of the past perfect follows:

I had spoken.	We had spoken.
He had spoken.	They had spoken.
You had spoken.	She had spoken.

The present perfect tense is used to denote that which took place in the past but has consequence extending into the present. *Example*: I have completed my work (the action of completing is past. The consequence extending into the present is that I need not work any more because I have completed).

The conjugation of the present perfect tense follows:

I have spoken.	We have spoken.
He has spoken.	They have spoken.
You have spoken.	She has spoken.

The future perfect tense is used to denote that which will occur before a specific moment in the future. By the time you arrive tomorrow (the specific moment in the future) I shall have completed my work (the action that will have occurred before a specific moment in the future).

The conjugation of the future perfect follows.

I shall have completed.	We shall have completed.
He will have completed.	They will have completed.
You will have completed.	She will have completed.

The 'principal parts' of verbs are also important. The principal parts are simply the forms of the verbs used with various tenses. They are past particple, past and present.

The past participle is used as part of the verb phrases for the three perfect tenses (present perfect, past perfect, future perfect).

I have sung. (present perfect)

I had sung. (past perfect)

I shall have sung. (future perfect)

The past form is used to form the past tense (this is also called imperfect).

Yesterday I sang. (past tense)

The present form is used with the present tense but it is also used as part of the verb phrases in the future tense

Today I sing. (present tense)

Tomorrow I shall sing. (future tense)

In the table below principal parts of certain verbs have been listed

	Present	Past	Past participle
1.	Come	Came	Come
2.	Bring	Brought	Brought
3.	Catch	Caught	Caught
4.	Begin	Began	Begun
5.	Break	Broke	Broken
6.	Arise	Arose	Arisen
7.	Do	Did	Done
8.	Draw	Drew	Drawn
9.	Eat	Ate	Eaten
10.	Fall	Fell	Fallen
11.	Know	Knew	Known
12.	Give	Gave	Given
13	G[illegible]	[illegible]	Gone

15. Lie (Recline)	Lay	Lain
16. Lose	Lost	Lost
17. Raise	Raised	Raised
18. Ring	Rang	Rung
19. Rise	Rose	Risen
20. See	Saw	Seen
21. Sing	Sang	Sung
22. Sit	Sat	Sat
23. Steal	Stole	Stolen
24. Swim	Swam	Swum
25. Take	Took	Taken
26. Tear	Tore	Torn
27. Throw	Threw	Thrown
28. Write	Wrote	Written
29. Wear	Wore	Worn
30. Speak	Spoke	Spoken

One has to be careful with the following principal parts of verbs that can be difficult.

1. Bid (command) - present
   Bade - past
   Bidden - past participle
2. Bid (offer) - present
   Bid - past
   Bid - past participle
3. Hang (suspend) - present
   Hung - past
   Hung - past participle
4. Hang (execute) - present
   Hanged - past
   Hanged - past participle

If there is a shifting of tense the meaning also changes. See the following examples.

Wrong: Last year when I am down in Tokyo, he tells the boss a lie.

Right: Last year when I was down in Tokyo, he told the boss a lie.

Wrong: When I come home at night, he will be reading his newspaper.

Right: When I come home at night, he is reading his newspaper.

While expressing a general truth and a historical present, the present tense must be used.

Examples

Last month our priest reminded us that living the upright life is a discipline (general truth).

Jawaharlal Nehru is one of the great leaders in our history (historical present).

Jawaharlal Nehru <u>is</u> one of the great leaders in our history Historical event hence Present Tense 'is' used. Historical Present

One should be careful not to get confused between *imperfect tense* and *present perfect*. Present perfect tense is used to express action completed in the past with consequence extending into the present; imperfect tense however is used to express an indefinite past.

The other important component of a verb is the *voice*. One must be careful in using the voice. First let us learn:

Active Voice	**Passive Voice**
In this the subject of the sentence performs the action.	In this the subject is acted upon.
Gopi paints the house.	The house is being painted.

Though shifting from active to passive voice within the sentence or the paragraphs is accepted by some, others insist that such shifts should be avoided. It is important that one maintains a single voice and avoids shifting (active to passive or vice versa) to maintain the clarity of a sentence or paragraph.

Split Infinitives and Split Verbs – The infinitive is the 'to' form of verb. *To drive, to sing, to run*. If a word is placed between the two words in the infinitive (e.g. *to quickly finish*) the infinitive is said to be split.

Wrong: Mrs. Sharma always likes to *closely examine* every report.

Right: Mrs. Sharma always likes to *examine closely* every report.

Sometimes an infinitive simply must be split to gain the meaning intended.

Example: Visitors are asked to please leave their belongings away from the main hall.

Here the word 'please' must be placed within the infinitive so that it may modify the whole idea of being kind enough to leave the belongings away from the main hall.

When a verb is composed of two or more words, the parts should not be split, if such a splitting can be avoided. Occasionally, however the verb must be split.

Example: Vidya *was* never *cooking* at the right time (here splitting is right).

Wrong: Mr. Gopal did, I feel certain, speak on that topic before (splitting to be avoided).

Right: Mr. Gopal did speak, I feel certain, on that topic before.

Let us now consider the 'mood' of the verb. It refers exclusively to verbs. Mood is the property of the verb which reflects the manner in which the user conceives the verb. For example, if one wants to state an actual fact, one uses the indicative mood.

Example: He is the principal.

The horse trots slowly around the track.

Subjunctive mood is used to express a wish; express a condition contrary to actual fact. The present subjunctive is conjugated as follows:

I were	We were
He were	They were
You were	You were

Examples

I wish she *were* there. (expresses a wish)

If she *were* here, she would help us. (expresses a condition contrary to actual fact.)

Wrong: I wish I was as tall as my father.

Right: I wish I were as tall as my father.

Wrong: If Gita was here now, she would show you how to paint.

Right: If Gita were here now, she would show you how to paint.

(×) I wish I was as tall as my father.
(✓) I wish I were as tall as my father.

When a speaker or writer wants to predicate a statement upon a hypothesis, he uses a subjunctive mood to establish the hypothesis (i.e., *the situation contrary to fact*) and he uses conditional mood to express his statement (i.e., *the statement predicated upon the assumption*).

Example

If I were home, I should be sleeping.

The verb 'were' is subjunctive.

The verb phrases 'should be sleeping' is conditional.

To use the conditional mood correctly a condition contrary to fact must be involved. If no such condition is present a 'false conditional' results. This is a common error.

Wrong: Everyday when I arrived, she would be at her desk.

Right: Everyday when I arrived, she was at her desk.

To express situations involving obligation or duty forms, such word as 'must', 'should', 'ought' are used.

We must reach our target.

I should clean the room today.

He ought to help his friend.

Sometimes a common error arises due to the use of an indicative to express duty/obligation.

Wrong: If he comes, do I tell him to stay back?

Right: If he comes, should I tell him to stay back?

There can be some miscellaneous errors in the use of verbs. One is a tendency to curtail verbs by dropping a letter or a syllable.

Wrong: She never expects us to come.

Right: She never expected us to come.

In some localities certain verbs are used in a different pattern, creating localisms.

Example: We will *doze (bull doze)* the debris.

There is also confusion in the use of 'don't' and 'doesn't'. There are contracted forms of *do not* and *does not*. One can substitute the full form for the contracted form.

Wrong: The baby don't look like his father.

Right: The baby doesn't look like his father.

While using verbs one must keep in mind that the arrangement of verbs in a sentence should be logical, i.e., that of the actual sequence of events.

Wrong: She ate, dressed and washed before nine o'clock. (wrong unless this was the order of procedure).

Right: She washed, dressed and ate before nine o'clock.

30

MORE DOUBTS AND SOLUTIONS

1. What do the terms 'caveat emptor' and 'brinkmanship' mean? How are they used? 'Caveat emptor' is a Latin phrase meaning 'let the buyer beware'. Put simply, this means that the supplier has no legal obligation to inform buyers about any defects in his goods or services. The onus is on the buyer to determine for himself or herself that the goods or services is satisfactory. This term used in sales industry is often misunderstood and misinterpreted.

   Generally speaking, the practice of treading a political or business path with catastrophic consequences right up to the brink of disaster and managing to desist or manoeuvre things to one's advantage just before one's downfall is called brinkmanship. This term is used for extremely capable people or persons in the corporate field or the arena of politics. Care should be taken to restrict its use to such context only.

2. The word 'bunk' (noun) means: shelf-like bed. The word bunk in the meaning of nonsense is a shortened form of *bumkum*, a variant of *buncombe* which in turn is the name of a country in the North Carolina. Around 1820 a congressman by the name of Pelix Walker who represented the district in which Buncombe county, North Carolina, was located, had stubbornly persisted in delivering an exceptionally long and wearisome speech to the 16th congress despite the objections of his impatient colleagues. He later explained that he had been determined "to make

a speech for Buncombe". Buncombe as well as its variant Bumkum quickly caught on as a synonym for meaningless political claptrap.

3. What is the origin and meaning of the phrase 'red herring'? Sometimes when you are talking to someone, he/she asks you some very embarrassing questions. What do you normally do in these circumstances? You say something which you hope will distract his attention. You try to get the individual to talk about something else. This ploy that you use to divert the individual's attention is called a red herring. A red herring is normally used by people to divert the attention of others from something important. Who are the people who are well known for introducing a red herring every now and then? Politians of course!

Examples

1. The detectives followed all the leads but unfortunately they were all red herrings.
2. The minister said that he would not answer the question because it involved national security, but that was a red herring to avoid a discussion of the terrible mistakes he had made.
3. The debate was really getting interesting when unfortunately one of the questions the panelist raised proved to be a bit of a red herring.

A herring is a kind of fish; it turns red only when it is 'cured', that is, when it is smoked and salted; the fish emits a very strong smell. In the past the criminals made use of it to help them in their bid to escape. Convicts used the herring to help them throw dogs off the scent. Since the herring had a very strong smell the police dogs followed the scent of the herring rather than that of the escaped convict. The original expression was "drag a red herring across the tail" but now it has been reduced to red herring.

4. 'Onometapoeia' is a word that imitates the sound it represent, for example, splash, wow, gush, kerplumk are such words. Such devices bring out the full flavour of words. Comparison and association are sometimes strengthened by syllables which imitate or reproduce the sound they describe. When this occurs it is called onometapoeia (a Greek word meaning name-making) for the sounds literally make the meanings in such words as buzz, crash, whirr, clang, hiss, purr, squeak, mumble, hush, boom.
5. 'Sabbath' and 'Shibboleth' are often confused with each other. Sabbath is the day of rest from work (Saturday for Jenes, Sunday for Christians). 'Shibboleth' – This word has a complex origin. In Hebrew it may mean 'an ear of grain' or 'a stream'. This word is from the *Book of Judges* (12:6, authorised version). In English, shibboleth was borrowed from a passage from this book and has come to mean a use of language or custom regarded as distinctive of the members of a particular group. From this it has also developed the sense of a slogan or catchword used by a particular group.

31

USE OF ADJECTIVES AND ADVERBS

A predicate adjective is an adjective in the part of the sentence from the verb onward when the sentence is arranged in its natural order (the predicate) which modifies a noun or pronoun acting as the subject of the verb.

Example: The milk tasted sweet (*sweet* modifies *milk*).

Here *sweet* is the predicate objective, *milk* is the noun, which is the subject of the verb *tasted*.

There can be confusion in using expression 'due to'. Here the word 'due' must be a predicate adjective. 'Due to' cannot be used as a synonym to 'because of' which does the work of a preposition (hence a proportional construction).

Wrong: The highways were slippery due to snow.
Right: The highways were slippery because of snow.

The expression 'prior to' is similar to the expression 'due to', ('prior' must be a predicate adjective like 'due'). 'Prior to' cannot be used as a synonym to 'before' and 'prior to' cannot be used to start a sentence.

Wrong: The card came prior to the gift.
Right: The card came before the gift.

Sensory verbs is one which pertains to the senses (seeing, tasting, smelling, hearing, feeling). When using a modifier after a sensory verb one must be careful with one's choice.

Example

She looked sad.

The predicate adjective modifies the subject pronoun *she*.

(X) The card came prior to the gift.

(✓) The card came before the gift.

Example

She looked sadly about the room. (This is also correct; 'sadly' is an adverb modying the verb 'looked').

The following sentences show the use of predicate adjective after sensory verbs.

Examples

The flower smells sweet.

The milk tastes sweet.

Wrong: She feels badly about the defeat (needs a predicate adjective).

Right: She feels bad about the defeat.

Linking verbs are *am, is, are, was, be,* etc. (forms of verb 'to be'). *Seem, became, turned*, etc., link the subject to other words. A linking verbs do not refer to something which the subject does or experience. Linking verb is usually followed by a predicate adjective, and once we can recognise a linking verb, handling a predicate adjective becomes easy.

Example: She became strong and reliable.

Became – linking verb; strong, reliable – predicate adjectives – modifies the pronoun *she*.

Differentiating Adjectives and Adverbs

To avoid the various errors in the use of adjectives and adverbs one must know the clear-cut definitions of adverb and adjective; one must know the appropriate adjectival and adverbial forms of the various words and must be able to fit them in their proper forms.

Adjective	Adverb
a word that modifies (tells something of the quality or limits in some way) a noun or pronoun.	a word that modifies a verb, adjective or another adverb.

Confusion arises from misinterpreting one for the other (adjectival and adverbial forms)

Example

1. The tired, beaten team retired to the locker room.
   Tired, beaten modify the noun *team*.
2. She works rapidly.
   (*Rapidly* modifies the verb *works*).

Bad is an adjective, *badly* is an adverb.

Easy is an adjective, *easily* is an adverb.

Quick is an adjective, *quickly* is an adverb.

Real is an adjective, *really* is an adverb.

Some is an adjective, *somewhat* is an adverb.

Good is an adjective, *well* is an adverb.

Slow is an adjective, *slowly* is an adverb.

See the following examples for the correct use of adjectives and adverbs

ADJECTIVES

Wrong: He is becoming strong everyday.
Right: He is becoming stronger everyday.

Wrong: He is a coward man.
Right: He is a cowardly man.

Wrong: You are more wiser than he.
Right: You are wiser than he.

Adverb

Wrong: He plays good.
Right: He plays well.

Wrong: He can read this book more quick than I.
Right: He can read this book more quickly than I.

Wrong: He spoke very hasty.
Right: He spoke very hastily.

From the above explanations and examples one can easily differentiate between an adjective and adverb. The correct form to be used in the correct instance must be the rule.

Adverbial modifiers are used by some when a substantive (noun, pronoun) is needed. An adverb gets used in place of a noun/pronoun. A case of mistaken identity!

Wrong: My greatest thirst is when I work hard in the strong sun ('Thirst' is a noun, and cannot be equated with "When I work hard in the strong sun" which is an adverbial phrases).

Right: My greatest thirst comes when I work hard in a strong sun.

✕ my greatest thirst is when I work hard in a strong sun.
✓ my greatest thirst comes when I work hard in a strong sun.

When and *where* are generally adverbs. Consequently they cannot be used to introduce noun clauses.

Wrong: Now is when he should be on hand.

Right: Now is the time when he should be on hand.

Wrong: Erosion is where the soil is washed away.

Right: Erosion occurs when the soil is washed away.

The adverb *where* must not be used for the relative pronoun *that;* when the adverb *where* is used interrogatively it should not be accompanied by the preposition *at*. Note the following examples.

Wrong: I see in this book where the city of Bangalore has a large garden.

Right: I see in this book that the city of Bangalore has a large garden.

Wrong: Where did you see the lion at when you were hunting?

Right: Where did you see the lion when you were hunting?

The word *why* is an adverb. The expression *what for* must not be used as a substitute for the adverb *why*.

Wrong: What for did you paint the house pink?

Right: Why did you paint the house pink?

The adverb *why* should not be used for the relative pronoun *that*.

Wrong: This is the reason *why* I am writing.

Right: This is the reason *that* I am writing.

× This is the reason why I am writing.
✓ This is the reason that I am writing.

There is a situation in which *why* is part adverb and part conjunction. This situation is called conjunctive adverb. See the following examples:

I never know *why* he came.

The ministers explained *why* he was not interested in the plan.

Therefore while using *why* one should also keep in mind this concept of (adverb + conjunction role of *why*) it.

32

MODIFYING ELEMENTS

In this section we will be discussing errors relating to modifying elements, prepositions and conjunctions. We will also very briefly discuss errors in making comparisons.

Modifying elements are words and group of words which describe or limit. These are important in the meaning of sentences. Whenever possible modifiers should be arranged according to length with the shortest coming first. Following this one can add the other modifiers.

Example: She was dishevelled, dirty and untidy.

Here the modifiers are not in sequence. *Dirty* should come first followed by the others.

She was dirty, untidy and dishevelled.

A logical sequence is important in the arrangement of modifiers.

Example: As the weeks wore on, she became tired, bored and exhausted (this is wrong because she probably became bored before she became tired). Note the logical sequence in the following rewritten sentences.

As the weeks wore on she became *bored, tired* and *exhausted.*

Some modifiers have a distinctly negative meaning and hence they should not be used as modifiers of another negative word. Such a situation may create a double negative.

Example

Wrong: They can't hardly speak Hindi.

Right: They can hardly speak Hindi.

Sometimes a thought is expressed incorrectly due to wrong use of modifiers.

Example

Wrong: Before she was born, Gita's uncle decided to change his will in favour of Gita.

Right: Before Gita was born, her uncle decided to change his will in her favour.

In using single words as modifiers one should be careful. Care must be taken to see that they modify the proper word. If not there will be a grammatically correct sentence but the meaning will be changed.

Wrong: The shopkeeper nearly lost two hundred parcels in the fire.

Right: The shopkeeper lost nearly two hundred parcels in the fire.

(This implies the shopkeeper lost almost two hundred parcels.)

The above two sentences are grammatically acceptable but difference in the position of the word the 'nearly' brings out different meanings.

Misplaced modifying clauses and phrases can be corrected by changing their position or by recasting the sentence.

Wrong: It was the third cake on the plate *that she ate*.

Right: She ate the third cake on the plate.

Wrong: She told me what to do *with a smile*.

Right: She told me *with a smile* what to do.

Dangling and squinting modifiers need a mention. A 'dangling modifier' refers to the modifier which does not function properly because one or more words have been omitted.

Wrong: Walking down the road, a hotel was seen.

Right: Walking down the road, I saw a hotel.

Right: As I walked down the road, I saw a hotel.

A 'squinting modifier' is one which can modify either of the two elements between which it is placed.

Example: The aroma of the coffee that she was preparing slowly became noticeable.

'Slowly' is the adverb which modifies either the idea of preparing or the idea of becoming noticeable. The adverb attempts to look or squint in two directions.

(×) she told me what to do with a smile.
(✓) she told me with a smile what to do.

Prepositions are words used with a noun or pronoun to show position, time or means (e.g., at home, by train). In olden days the practice of ending sentences with a preposition was strictly objected to. Now it has become acceptable to avoid awkward sentence structure.

Example: The watchman seemed to know what the sign stood for.

The following sentences illustrate instances where the ending of a sentence with a preposition can be avoided.

Example

1. Whom should I give the packet to?
   To whom should I give the packet? (this is better)
2. This is the table I am planning to put the ashtray on.
   This is the table on which I am planning to put the ashtray.

A preposition is usually placed before a noun or pronoun that it governs.

Example: Many people die of heart disease every year.

In the following sentences note the exception to the above rule. We see a preposition being placed at the end of a sentence when the relative pronoun is 'that'; when a preposition governs a relative pronoun; when the relative pronoun is understood.

1. The baby tore the paper that I was drawing on.
2. This is the girl whom I spoke about.
3. This is the man (whom) she spoke to (whom is understood).

Preposition can be placed at the end of a sentence when it governs an interrogative pronoun or adverb.

Examples: What are you gazing at? (interrogative pronoun)

Where are you going to? (interrogative adverb)

A preposition can be placed at the beginning of a sentence also.

Example: To whom did you give my book?

There are occasions when the preposition *for, from, in, on*, are omitted before nouns of place or time.

Example: Wait a minute (wait for a minute).

One should also know that there are many words which can be used both as a preposition and as an adverb.

Examples

1. She was here before nine (*before* is used as a preposition).
2. She has done this sort of work before (*before* is adverb).

A suspended prepositional phrase occurs when a given noun or pronoun serves as the object of two prepositions. The meaning of the first prepositional phrase is not clear until the end the second phrase is reached.

Example: We are interested in and indebted to the lady.

While using suspended prepositional phrases one must guard against omitting either of the prepositions.

The words 'and indebted' is to suspend the preposition 'in' from its object 'lady'.

Wrong: She had a need and interest in athletics. (wrong because no preposition is stated after 'need'; it is assumed to be 'in').

Right: She had a need for and an interest in athletics.

The double preposition can be sometimes correct and sometimes incorrect.

Example

She came over to the house (correct use of double preposition). Sometimes these are not considered as double prepositions. They are termed 'phrasal propositions' – the first is considered to be an adverb and the second one a preposition.

The preposition 'of' is often incorrectly used with verbs. One must avoid such errors.

Wrong: Keep off of the grass.
Right: Keep off the grass.

'Of' is also misused as a substitute for 'have'. This should be avoided.

Wrong: I could of had two more assistants.
Right: I could have had two more assistants.

The preposition 'up' is often unnecessarily used with verbs.

Wrong: Mrs. Gupta is planning to do up her house. (colloquial)
Right: Mrs. Gupta is planning to decorate her house.

In case 'up' is used with verbs care should be taken to keep it with the verb and not needlessly separate it from the verb.

Wrong: The mechanic tuned the motor *up*.
Right: The mechanic tuned *up* the motor.

There are often doubts regarding the use of prepositions. With verb 'blame', the doubt is whether it should be blame 'on' or blame 'it on'.

Wrong: Please don't blame it on Sharma.
Right: Please don't blame Sharma.
Wrong: He blamed the accident on Gupta.
Right: He blamed Gupta for the accident.

Another common source of confusion is in the use of 'differ from-differ with' and 'different from-different than'.

Example: 'Differ from' means to be 'dissimilar'.

This picture differs from that one.

Example: 'Differ with' means to 'disagree with someone'.

I differ with Mrs. Lalitha on that question.

Wrong: Mrs. Sharma differs from Mrs. Gupta on that point

(wrong if disagreement is meant, right if dissimilarity is meant).

Right: Mrs. Sharma differs with Mrs. Gupta on that point.

Different from – here 'from' is a preposition.

Example: *This painting is different from that painting*.

Here the preposition 'from' is needed to establish the relationship between the word painting (the second painting) and the word 'different'. If, on the other hand, 'from' is replaced by the conjunction 'than', we will have the above sentence read like this:

This painting is different than that painting is different.

This sentence does not make any sense, therefore the first sentence with *different from* is the correct one.

Right: My house is different from your house in many ways.
Right: My house differs from your house in many ways.

Certain prepositions are used with certain ideas.

'At' is used in the following ways:

1. In speaking of things at rest.
2. Before villages and small towns; *at home, at school*.
3. Before big towns when one stays there for a short time on the way to some other place.

   While going to Chennai, I shall stay at Madurai for a day or two.
4. Before a noun that shows a relation of time, age, stage or condition.

   At my disposal; at the age of seven; at ten.
5. To show the rates of things.

   At ten rupees per kilogram.

'In' is used in the ways mentioned below:

1. Before countries, provinces, districts, large towns.
2. With the names of year and month.

   In 1987, in March 1966.

3. Before the noun denoting time, state or point of reference.
   In my opinion, in an hour, in distress.
4. To denote position or rest with in a space.
   In the examination hall, in bed.

'On' is used:

1. For things at rest: *Two pots are on the table.*
2. To denote concern and support: *I wrote a book on art.*
3. Before the names of days and dates: *On Tuesday, on the sixth of March.*
4. To express a condition or situation: *The poor woman is on the verge of starvation.*
5. 'Upon' is used in speaking of things in motion: *The dog pounced upon the boy.*

'In to' is used:

1. To denote movement from outside to inside.
   A girl fell into the river.
2. To indicate change from one state to another.
   He will translate it into German.
3. *Between* is used for two persons or things.
   Among is used for more than two persons or things.
   Above means more than a certain sum.

Example: The price of this picture is above hundred rupees.

The dog pounced upon the boy.
Note: Upon is used in speaking of things in motion.

'By' is used:

1. According to.
   It is eight by my watch.
2. To show measure.
   Wire is sold by the metre.
3. To show the manner of an action.
   I seized her by the hair.

4. To show nearness of place or time.
She asked me to sit by her.

'With' is used to:

1. Denote the instrument with which an action is performed.
He was badly beaten with a big stick.
2. In the sense of saying despite, in spite of.
With all his faults, she loves him.
3. To denote company.
He went there with me.

The following sentences show how to use 'at' and avoid 'with'.

Wrong: I was angry with the result.
Right: I was angry at the result.

In the following sentences note how 'with' is used.

Wrong: I was angry at my sister.
Right: I was angry with my sister.

Remember the Rule

One becomes angry *with* persons but *at* situations.

'Beside' is used to mean:

1. At the side of; close to; near and also.
2. To compare with: *You are quite tall beside your elder brother.*

Beside is also used to mean in addition to and to express something at the end one's self-control.

Example: *He was beside himself with joy.*

'Till' means up to, as late as:

Example: I work daily from morning till night.

'Since' as a preposition is used for time, never for place. It is used with a point in time. It is often used with the perfect tense. 'Since' means from that time to the time of speaking. *She has been here since Monday* (from Monday till now).

While using 'to' and 'with' in the context of comparing an object one should be careful.

Right: I am comparing this shirt with that shirt.

Right: I am comparing this shirt to that shirt.

In the strict sense, the word 'to', when used with numbers, does not include the second number stated.

Wrong: If one is asked to count from one to five, he should count as follows: one, two, three, four, *five*.

Right: If one is asked to count from one to five, he should count as follows: one, two, three, four.

Right: If one is asked to count from *one to five inclusive*, he should count as follows: one, two, three, four, five.

When used with verbs denoting speech (*talk*, *speak*. etc) the preposition, 'to' indicates that one person did all the speaking. The preposition 'with', on the other hand, conveys the idea of at least a two-way discussion. Note the following sentences which illustrate the above concept.

Examples

1. I spoke to the team. (here 'I' did all the talking.)
2. I spoke with the team about their training. (Here the discussion between the speaker and the team is conveyed.)

(✓) **I am comparing this shirt with that shirt.**
(✓) **I am comparing this shirt to that shirt.**

1. While using a preposition:
   a. Occasionally a redundancy occurs with the use of two prepositions in the same phrase.
   'Over and above political trends'.
   b. 'On' and 'to' (prepositions, are used in a sentence together, a doubt arises as to whether one should place them as one word or as two single words.

We drove on to the village.

Here 'on' is an adverb (it modifies *drove*).

'To' is a preposition (shows the relationship between the verb 'drove' and noun 'village'). The rule is when 'on' is an adverb and 'to' is a preposition write them as separate words.

We drove *onto* the bridge.

Here *onto* is a preposition and hence written as a single word because it shows the relationship between 'drove' and 'bridge'.

2. There are some words with a preposition which require a gerund after them.

Examples: bent upon doing

insist on going

tired of writing

prevent from working

fond of playing

3. There are some words which differ slightly in form and meaning and are formed from the same word. Then they take a different preposition after them.

Examples:

according to	but	in accordance with
affection for	but	affectionate to
dislike to	but	liking for
alternate with	but	alternative to
hinder from	but	hindrance to
equal to	but	equally with

Conjunctions

A word that connects other words is called a conjunction. There should be proper use of the correlative conjunctions "as...as" and "so...as" while speaking and writing. "As...as" should be used in a positive situation and "so...as" in a negative situation.

Wrong: She is not as tall as her mother.
Right: She is not so tall as her mother.
Right: Arun is as strong as Varun.
Right: Mohan is as capable as Sohan.

While using correlative conjunctions "as...as" one must be careful not to omit the second 'as'.

Wrong: This table is as good if not better than the old one.
Right: This table is as good as, if not better, than the old one.

While using 'as' one should be careful as to avoid substituting it for 'that' or whether'.

Wrong: I am not sure as he is the man we need.
Right: I am not sure whether (or that) he is the man we need.

While using 'either...or' and 'neither…nor', one should not interchange the counterparts: 'Either' should be with 'or' and 'neither' with 'nor'.

Note the following examples.

Right: Neither Arun nor I am going.
Right: Either Gita or Sita must join the debate.

One should remember that the verb following the second noun or pronoun always agrees in person and number with the noun preceding it. Note the following examples.

Neither Arun nor I am capable.

Neither Arun nor he is capable.

Neither they nor we are capable.

The words 'either' and 'neither' should be used only when the number of persons/ideas involved is two. If it is more than two persons/ideas 'either' and 'neither' should not be used.

Right: Neither the car nor the motorcycle will be there.
Wrong: Neither the car, the motorcycle, nor the bicycle will be there.

For expressing the things we can say.

The car, the motorcycle and/or the bicycle will not be there.

(Here we are not using 'either').

When a pronoun has as its antecedent as a noun or pronoun located in an 'either...or' or a 'neither...nor' construction the second named noun or pronoun is considered the antecedent. The second named noun or pronoun therefore governs the person and the number of the following pronoun.

Wrong: Neither Paul nor Oscar was in *their* place.
Right: Neither Paul nor Oscar was in *his* place.

We have discussed several points regarding the use of 'either' and 'neither' certain other words also raise doubt in relation to their use as conjunctions. The word 'except' is generally either a preposition or a verb. It is never a conjunction.

Wrong: Arun does not eat except it is dinner time.
Right: Arun does not eat unless it is dinner time.

Like the word 'except', 'like' is also either a verb or a preposition. It is never a conjunction.

Wrong: She runs like I do (wrong because like is used as a conjunction).
Right: She runs as I do.

The word 'than' is a conjunction. One must be careful to supply the words that are understood (if any) after it.

Wrong: I have more mistakes in my report than him.
Right: I have more mistakes in my report than he has.

The subordinate conjunction 'if' conveys the idea of a condition. It should not be confused with the subordinate conjunction 'whether' or the relative pronoun 'that'.

Wrong: Mother wants to know if Arun has arrived.
Right: Mother wants to know whether Arun has arrived.
Wrong: We are not sure if she is going.
Right: We are not sure that she is going.

'Without' is a preposition. It must not be used as a conjunction.

Wrong: Gopal will not follow the order without the vice-captain tells him.

Right: Gopal will not follow the order unless the vice-captain tells him.

Before we end the discussion we must mention a few points regarding comparisons. We have three degrees of comparison.

	Positive Degree	Comparative Degree	Superlative Degree
1.	This is the first in the hierarchy of compartive degrees	Second	Third
2.	It is used in speaking of one person, idea or object only.	It is used in speaking of two persons, ideas or objects.	It is used in speaking of three persons, ideas or objects.

Examples

She is a slow worker.	She is a slower worker than Lakshmi.	She is the slowest of the workers.

There are various errors in making comparisons. The most common errors are degrees of comparison.

Wrong: This is the least expensive of the two jewels.
Right: This is the less expensive of the two jewels.
Wrong: She is the prettiest twin.
Right: She is the prettier twin.

When making comparisons one must ensure that it conveys the appropriate meaning.

Wrong: Ram is taller than any boy in the class. (This sentence is wrong, if Ram is a member of the class. However, this sentence is right if Ram is not a member of the class).
Right: Ram is taller than any other boy in the class.
Right: Paris is larger than any city in Brazil. (Right because Paris is not in Brazil).

An absolute is an adjective or an adverb which cannot be compared because it is complete. For example, the adjective 'square' is absolute because an object is either square or it is not; it cannot be more or most square.

To convey the idea that one object is closer to an absolute condition than the second object, the expression "more nearly" is employed.

Example

This table is more nearly square than that one. The expression less nearly is also employed.

Example

That table is less nearly square than this one.

Some common errors in the use of absolute adjectives are illustrated below.

1.Wrong: This desk is more circular than that one.
Right: This desk is more nearly circular than that one.

2.Wrong: Our work is the most vital in the entire project.
Right: Our work is the most important in the entire project.
Right: Our work is the most significant in the entire project.

3.Wrong: These bars are less parallel than those.
Right: These bars are less nearly parallel than those.

While using comparatives one must be cautious enough to avoid using double comparatives (using two comparatives) to make a single comparison. Such expressions often convey exaggerated meanings which are not needed.

Wrong: The old cycle moved much more faster than the new cycle (note the double comparative).
Right: The old cycle moved much faster than the new cycle.

Another error in comparison usages are 'false comparison'. There a comparative or a superlative degree construction is used without a clearly stated basis, i.e., the person, object or idea to which the second is being compared is not clear for the comparison.

Wrong: Arun is one of our better students.
Right: Arun is one of our superior students.

The speaker and the writer must be careful not to omit words which make a comparison incomplete or give a meaning other than the one intended. This leads to an incomplete comparison and a twisted meaning.

Wrong: I like him more than Gopal. (Here there is omission of words and the intended meaning is doubtful).
Right: I like him more than I like Gopal (if this is the meaning intended).
Right: I like him more than Gopal likes you (if this is the meaning intended).

Some incomplete comparisons are accepted in conversion but they should be avoided in writing.

Example: Vidya is not too intelligent (accepted in conversation).
Vidya is not superior in intelligence (to be used in writing).

One should also avoid the expression 'all the' combined with a comparative degree modifier (all the farther, all the faster) in formal English usages.

Wrong: Page thirty was all the farther he studied.
Right: He did not study beyond page thirty.

33

ERRORS IN PUNCTUATION

In this section we will be discussing errors in punctuation, redundancies, style, broad and vague words, and certain miscellaneous errors in usages.

Correct punctuation is more a part of common sense and necessity of expression than being a part of grammar rules. If there is no proper punctuation it can lead to misinterpretation of dialogue and sentences.

Note the following sentences with and without punctuation marks.

Comma (,)

1. Wrong: Gopal son of Jagjit came here.
   Right: Gopal, son of Jagjit, came here.
2. Wrong: She is not a stupid girl but is naive.
   Right: She is not a stupid girl, but is naive.
3. Wrong: Here is your towel mother please take it.
   Right: Here is your towel, mother, please take it.

Semicolon (;)

The semicolon is used when a greater pause is required.

1. The king's action did speak of this. Before the latest move, he had thrice dismissed elected governments. First it was the Sher Bahadur Deuba government in October 2001. Then the L.B. Chand government in early 2003 and thereafter the S.B. Thapa government in April 2003.

The above para has not used semicolon at appro-priate places.

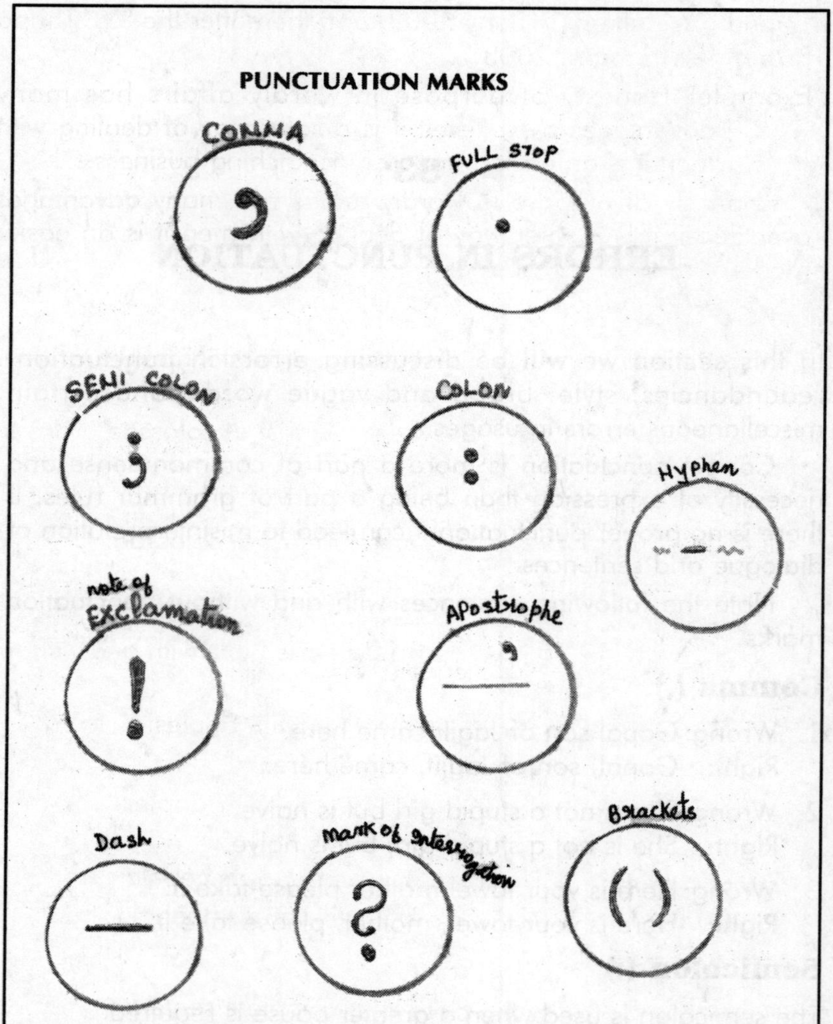

Now see the same para below with semicolons in proper places.

The king's action did speak of this. Before the latest move, he had thrice dismissed elected governments. First it was the Sher Bahadur Deuba govern-ment in October 2001; then the L.B.

Chand government in early 2003; and thereafter the S.B. Thapa government in April 2003.

Example: Honesty of purpose in wordly affairs has many advantages over deceit it is a safer way of dealing with men it is an easier made of dispatching business....

Honesty of purpose in wordly affairs has many advantages over deceit it is a safer way of dealing with men it is an easier mode of dispatching business;...

Colon (:)

The colon is used at the writer's discretion: to mark a greater pause than a semicolon; to introduce a clause, etc.

To the saints and true brothers in Christ at colossae grace to you and peace from.

God our father

To the saints and true brothers in Christ at colossae: grace to you and peace from.

God our father.

Look at the following excerpts from the *Bible* with and without colons.

1. Stay me with flagons, comfort me with apples.
   For I am sick of love.
   Stay me with flagons, comfort me with apples: for I am sick of love
2. My beloved is like a roe or a young hart behold, he...
   My beloved is like a roe or a young hart: behold, he...

Full Stop (.)

Full stop indicates the close of a complete sentence.

Example

Each fable is a miniature human drama (if we don't put a full stop we would be keeping the sentence abrupt).

Each fable is a miniature human drama.

The fables appeal at once to the young and the old

The fables appeal at once to the young and the old.

Note of Exclamation (!)

This is used to express an emotion, joy, anger, sorrow, feeling, etc.

Example

A great battle of Slivnitza A victory and it was won by Sergius.

A great battle of Slivnitza! A victory! and it was won by Sergius.

Note the above 'dialogue' by Catherine in Bernard Shaw's *Arms and the Man*. Note the emotion in the dialogue without and with the exclamatory mark.

1. I am so happy so proud
   I am so happy! so proud !
2. You dare
   You dare!
3. Devil Devil
   Devil ! Devil ! (note of '!' brings out the emotion of 'Curse' in these words).
4. Oh God! (shock)
5. Aha! (feeling of joy)
6. Ah, Guru! (feeling of relief)
7. Hey, Ram! (Exasperation)
8. Fire! Fire! (note the 'alarm' due to '!')
9. Wow! (Elation).
10. I! I!!! (gasping).
11. What a man! (admiration).
12. So I pawned it. I pawned it !!! (This reply with triple exclamation marks emphasizes the shock.)

Apostrophe (')

The apostrophe is used to denote that some letter or letters are missing.

1. Wrong: Ill say so.
   Right: I'll say so.

2. Wrong: Hes come to return the coat.
 Right: He's come to return the coat.
3. Wrong: Im like all the rest of them.
 Right: I'm like all the rest of them.

Interrogation (?)

This is used after sentences that ask questions.

1. Wrong: Is the library door shut
 Right: Is the library door shut?
2. Wrong: What could they do
 Right: What could they do?
3. Wrong: Have you ever seen the opera of Ernani
 Right: Have you ever seen the opera of Ernani?

How did the '?' originate? First at the end of each interrogative sentence the letters 'q' and 'o' of the word 'question' were written one below the other. Then to write quicker it became the symbol '?'. But the o below it never changed; hence '?' emerged thus.

Dash (—)

This marks a break or abrupt turn in a sentence.

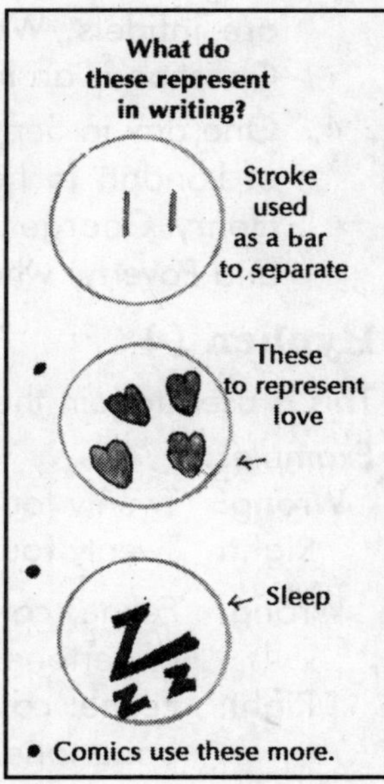

1. Tell them that if they stop to drink or tell stories if they are five minutes late they will have the skin taken off their backs.

   Tell them that—if they stop to drink or tell stories—if they are five minutes late, they will have the skin taken off their backs.

2. His sense of the sacredness of life, animal as well as human; his purity of living he ate no flesh, drank no alcohol, smoked no tobacco...

   His sense of the sacredness of life, animal as well as human; his purity of living—he ate no flesh, drank no alcohol, smoked no tobacco...

Brackets ()

Brackets are used like a couple of dashes for an interesting parenthetical phrase or sentence.

Example: He was the first to introduce a detailed description of scenery, furniture, stage properties and most important of all of the characters in the play. Very often....

He was the first to introduce a detailed description of scenery, furniture, stage properties and (most important of all) of the characters in the play. Very often....

Examples:

1. Tintoretto: Italian painter (1518-94), of the Venetian school...
2. He raises his eyebrows: a facial gesture expressing surprise or (sometimes) disapproval.
3. An infidel: one who does not believe in a particular religion. In the opinion of a Christian all non-Christian are infidels. While to (for example) a Mohammedan a Christian is an infidel or unbeliever.
4. One day in September 1884, he went to a hall in the city of London to hear a lecture by the American economist Henry George (author of a well-known book, *Progress and Poverty)* who advocated that national revenue...

Hyphen (-)

This is used to join the parts of a compound word.

Examples:

Wrong: Twenty four of them will hold twelve inside...
Right: Twenty-four of them will hold twelve inside...

Wrong: Feline: cat like; smooth speaking, but with a sinister undertone.
Right: Feline: cat-like; smooth speaking, but with a sinister undertone.

Wrong: He catches her by the shoulders and turns her face to face with him.
Right: He catches her by the shoulders and turns her face-to-face with him.
Wrong: Trumpet tongued lying.
Right: Trumpet-tongued lying.
Wrong: Half satisfied passions.
Right: Half-satisfied passions.
Wrong: Commander in chief.
Right: Commander-in-chief.
Wrong: ....both the serious and the humorous parts seem as fresh and up to date today as when he wrote...
Right: ....both the serious and the humorous parts seem as fresh and up-to-date to-day as when he wrote...

Before we close our discussion on punctuation we will learn some rules regarding their use.

1. There is no rule for the use of periods with abbreviations. In many common abbreviations the period is now omitted. Well-known organisations, agencies often omit the period.

Wrong: Mrs. Peter was active in the W.C.T.U.
Right: Mrs Peter was active in the WCTU (note period has been omitted).

2. If a question is to be rhetorical (for which no answer is expected) the exclamation mark may replace the question mark. *Was ever a boy so tormented !* (note ? is replaced by !)
3. The apostrope and 's' are added to singular and plural nouns to show possession.
   a. Ramu's book.
   b. Sharma's house.
   c. Aruna's bag.

   If however two or more persons constitute one object, only the second or last noun takes an apostrophe and 's'.

   a. Indra and Kumar's store.

b. Kavita, Kishore and Kreeti's office.

Apostrophe is omitted when the word becomes part of a proper noun.

Central Teachers College, Teamsters Union.

Apostrophe must be used to form the plurals of letters and numbers.

Wrong: There were five As in the word.
Right: There were five A's in the word.

The possessive pronouns (his, her, its, ours, yours, theirs, whose) never take the apostrophe.

Wrong: Who's bag is this?
Right: Whose bag is this?

4. A proper noun is always capitalised, while a common noun is not.

Wrong: Sam Smith drove his trick to port dixon, Malaysia.
Right: Sam Smith drove his truck to Port Dixon, Malaysia.

In a title, the first word and every succeeding "main" word is capitalised.

Wrong: She was reading *arms and the man*.
Right: She was reading *Arms and the Man*.

The names of fields of study which are derived from proper nouns are capitalised.

Wrong: She was studying german and greek.
Right: She was studying German and Greek.

The names of languages are always capitalised because they are derived from proper nouns.

5. In olden days all titles were set off by quotation marks ("). Now however main titles are italicised, while titles that are part of a larger work are set off by quotation marks.

Old – She was reading *Check Mate* from *A Twist in the Tale*.

New – She was reading "Check Mate" from *A Twist in the Tale*.

If a quotation appears within a quotation, the second quotation should be enclosed with single quotation mark.

6. Hyphen is generally used with prefix 'self' 'Post', 'ex', 'anti' and 'all'.

Wrong: Self centred self conscious self evident self possessed

Right: Self-centred self-conscious self-evident self-possessed

Wrong: all clear

Right: all-clear

Wrong: anti aircraft

Right: anti-aircraft

Certain words like attorney general, tonight, tomorrow, weakened, ill temper which were once hyphenated no longer require a hyphen.

'Today' this word was once hyphenated but is no longer hyphenated.

Certain hyphenated words drop the hyphen when they become predicate modifiers; *well-known, good-natured, ill-bred*.

Wrong: The actor was not always well-known.

Right: The actor was not always well known.

7. While using commas to punctuate dates and places, one must remember that when there is more than one element in the recording of a date or a place. The elements are separated from each other by commas. A common error is to omit the last comma.

Wrong: He chose Mumbai, India for his opening address on Monday, Feb 14, 2005 in order to reach a wide audience.

Right: He chose Mumbai, India, for his opening address on Monday, Feb. 14, 2005, in order to reach a wide audience.

'Common splice' describes a common error in current writing. The term refers to the practice of separating two sentences from each other by a comma rather than a period or semicolon. Common splice can be avoided by proper use.

Wrong: The highway was very slippery, snow was to be seen everywhere.

Right: The highway was very slippery; snow was to be seen everywhere.

8. Closed punctuation is the practice of adhering to strict guidelines for the use of punctuation. Open punctuation is the new trend. It is the tendency to deemphasize the use of commas and other punctuations.

   Gopal was ill, and naturally his work suffered. (open punctuation)

   Gopal was ill, and, naturally, his work suffered. (closed punctuation)

9. Newspapers, and magazines use individual punctuation marks stars, asterisks, heavy types as replacement for standard marks to gain special effects.

Labels which are produced in mass scales usually omit the punctuation marks but follow the capital letters.

Mr. GOPAL RATNA SHARMA
6034 ANDHERI
MUMBAI, INDIA

In the above label we see capital letters more probably to highlight the name and address which are important from mail/dispatch point of view.

Punctuation marks have been omitted.

MAOISTS GUN DOWN LAWYER

Note the heavy, bold type letters used in newspaper headlines to highlight the seriousness of the incident.

Free gift worth Rs 1000/- **
with every purchase
Buy a xxxpp computer
Rs 20,990/-*
**offer valid for limited period only.
* local taxes are applicable.

Note the above advertisement in a newspaper. The use of *double asterisks and stars* to highlight the salient features of their sale. One must be careful not to use these in excess and move away from the main issue.

'EATS, SHOOTS AND LEAVES: THE ZERO TOLERANCE APPROACH TO PUNCTUATION' – IN THE TITLE OF A BOOK BY LYNNE TRUSS.

This book has become a No.1 bestseller in London. Among the legions of the surprised are the executives at her publishing house, profile books, who ordered a modest initial printing of 15,000 books but now have 510,000 in print, and Truss' friends and family. When she was writing the book everybody thought it was commercial suicide to spend any time at all on it because it would not sell. Her mother even suggested that print a sticker on the front of book, "For the select few".

There are many possible reasons for the tremendous success of *Eats, Shoots and Leaves*. This book leads the reader through the valley of the shadow of comma splice, refers to the apostrophe as "our long suffering little friend"; makes a rousing case for the semicolons usefulness in among other things, "calling a bunch of brawling commas to attention" and describe Woodrow Wilson's inexplicable visceral hatred of the hyphen, which he called – spectacularly undermining his own argument – "the most un-American thing in the world."

The cover of this book makes a visual reference to a Panda-based joke about punctuation mishaps. The author says increasing number of people "don't know their apostrophe from their elbow". This book says, "Punctuation is quite a good system for making yourself clear and that it has been completely neglected by so many people."

The author has dedicated this book to the memory of the striking Bolshevik printers of St. Petersburg, who, Truss writers in 1905, demanded to be paid the same rate for punctuation marks as for letters, and thereby directly precipitated the first Russian Revolution.

The *Asian Age* tabloid has published a review of this book which gives many such interesting points on punctuation.

PUNCTUATION

How it is followed in Newspaper

SAARC / NO COLLABORATIVE PROJECT SO FAR: SARAN

"India cannot impose democracy on others"

see the use of / ; ""

irrigation projects eradicate poverty

see the use of ?

Jammu-Srinagar National Highway partially open

see the use of -

High drama as police perform Naxals' last rites

see the use of '

Palestine, Israel end hostilities

see the use of comma ,

Email: tecpool@vsnl.com

Ex Dip B.Sc/BE or any Grad

Email: ittabangalore@vsnl.net

www.timesjobs.com

@ represents at

look at the use of ; / . here

vsnl.net → here . stands for dot

timesjobs . com . means dot

"I will come back for deer counting next year too!"

see the use of ! "

20,000 Successful Students !

see the use of !

Health care... at home... just a call away...

see the use of ...

Pak. professor in Science City

see the use of (.)

PUNCTUATION

how it is used to
- ① bring out the piognancy in these quotes.
- ② bring out the piognancy in these quotes.
- ③ highlight a point
- ④ increase the curiesity & sell a product
- ⑤ comment on a decision

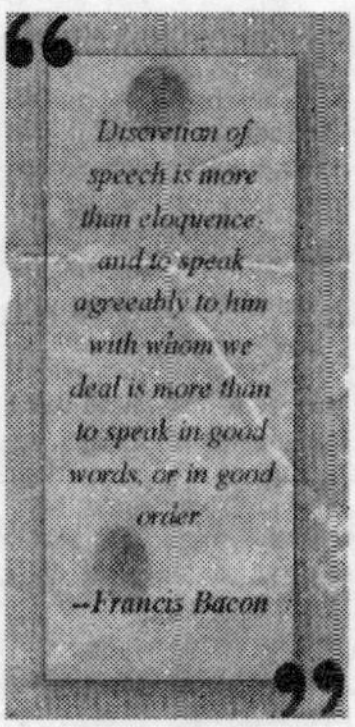

see the use “”

①

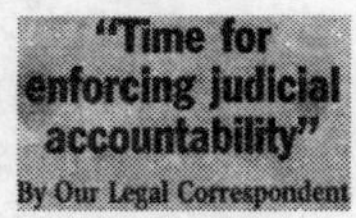

③ see the “ ” and the bold and thin letter

④

see the use of ? and * here

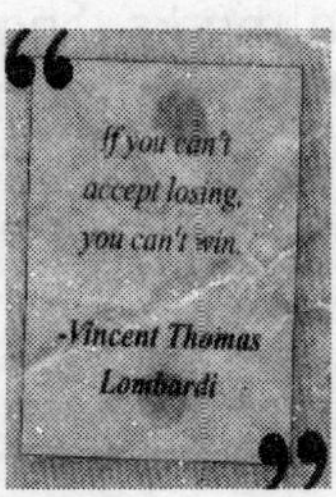

see the use of “”

②

⑤ see the wordings and the use of ‘.

Poets and authors have their own way of using words, punctuation and italics. These often violate the rules laid down by the standard grammar textbook. Style apart such violations are accepted as Poetic Licence.

Ordinarily italics are used for printing words that are to be emphasised but Bernard Shaw used instead spaced letters. Thus if the word glorious was to be emphasized in speaking the sentence "The world is really a glorious world" he would have it printed as g l o r i o u s, not glorious. This method not only avoided possible confusion with stage directions in italic type but it also represents what actually happens when we emphasize a word in speaking. We slow down our rate of speaking and the emphasized word occupies a longer time period, just as spaced word occupies more space on the paper when printed, but when the personal pronoun 'I' was to be emphasized, Shaw had to use the italic *I*.

Another peculiarity of Shaw's style of printing is the omission of apostrophe from construction such as Ive (usually printed as I've = I have), they ll (they' ll = They will), shant (shan't = shall not), em (em = them), wholl (who'll = who will), etc. This is sometimes confusing to the reader at first, but Shaw was thinking of the way in which these contractions are spoken.

It is important to know that Shaw did not use either quotation marks or italic type for the title or books of plays which he mentions in his preface to many of his plays. In ordinary printing all the titles would be in italic type or between quotation marks. Shaw rarely printed a list of the characters at the front of the play though this is customary in most other playwrights' printed works. He preferred that the reader should not be introduced to the characters by name until they appeared in the text of the play.

A redundancy is a word or expression that is in excess and thus makes a sentence weak or absurd. Redundancies are common in spoken and written English. Some redundancies have become acceptable as idioms.

Examples

1. Each and every person is responsible for his duties (a common redundancy).

2. Both Ravi and Arun are going (has become acceptable).

The term "any and all" is redundant because either of these words can convey the meaning by itself.

Wrong: Any and all of the flowers can be used in decoration.
Right: Any of the flowers can be used in decoration.
Right: All of the flowers can be used in decoration.

Certain other redundancies include: 'end result' ('result' conveys the thought of the 'end'); 'different kinds' ('kind' implies the word 'different'); 'equally as' ('as' used with the word 'equally' creates redundancy); 'individual person' ('individual' used with 'person' creates redundancy); 'people, person' (using these two words together creates redundancy).

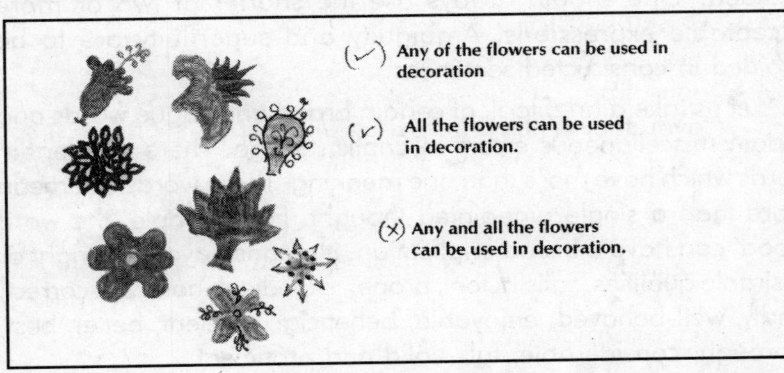

We have discussed punctuation and redundancies. Another aspect one should know is style. As a person writes or speaks over a long period he develops a characteristic choice and use of certain words, phrases and expressions. This is called his style. There can be a typical style of speaking and typical style of writing. If one is to have an error-free effective style he must check and improvise his writing and speaking. To evolve a good style one should:

1. Correct comma/uncommon error.
2. Enhance vocabulary.
3. Rectificy/reform grammatical mistakes.

4. Have modern thoughts, ideas, logic.
5. Make the expressions: speech, better, perfect, polished.
6. Refurbish the constructed statements/dialogue.
7. Edit the speech/manuscript to make it crisp and clear.

One must phrase similar ideas or elements in a sentence in a similar structural or grammatical form. The thoughts must be in a logical order. If two or more thoughts are to be joined by coordinate conjunctions they should be related. The sentences should be simple and unnecessary words should be omitted if the sentence looks and sounds 'word heavy'. If a compound sentence is used to express two ideas, the ideas are to be coordinated or given equal importance. Unnecessary repetition of the word is to be avoided. One should always use the shorter of two or more acceptable expressions. Ambiguity and superfluity are to be avoided in constructed sentences.

Let us take a brief look at certain broad and vague words and certain miscellaneous errors in English usage. There are certain words which have more than one meaning. These words can mean more than a single pinpointed thought. For example, the word 'good' can have a broad implication. It means having the right or desirable qualities, satisfactory, proper, expedient, normally correct, kindly, well-behaved, enjoyable, beneficial, efficient, better, best, thorough, considerable, full, valid and proficient.

Since such a word encompasses such a broad meaning one must be careful in using such words.

Words like big, break, calm, claim, change, close, get, go, important, office, station (can mean a police, railway, bus, petrol – any of these stations), make, bad, hit, worker (can mean any work), thing, well, old, pass, sign, run, rule have broad connotations.

While using such words one should be careful and consider all the meanings conveyed by that word. If there is a single alternative word to convey one's thought (apart from these words) he should use that word. The meaning conveyed should not be vague but should be precise (a worker can be a social worker; factory worker; worker bee; etc.).

Certain miscellaneous errors in usage of English are often accepted as idioms. As far as possible one should stick to speaking/conversing/writing error-free, grammatically correct English. Under the miscellaneous errors:

1. One common error is the needless use of word 'also'. If not needed, it should be avoided

Wrong: The boy ate chips, biscuit and also fruit.
Right: The boy ate chips, biscuit and fruit.

2. Using double negative words must be avoided. The double negative is the use of two negatives to express a single negative idea.

Wrong: Ravi doesn't want none of that cake.
Right: Ravi doesn't want any of that cake.

3. When a person is given two or more titles be careful not to let one title repeat. Double titling is a common error and should be avoided.

Wrong: We spoke with Engr: Ravi B.E.
Right: We spoke with Engr: Ravi (Engineer and B.E means the e same and hence one is enough).

While using Dr. (doctor) one should be careful as to whether it is a medical Dr. (MBBS) or a Doctorate (Phd).

4. The use of the abbreviation 'etc.' or the longer form etcetera is still not well accepted in formal writing. It is a broad and vague term. It is based on the assumption that the reader knows exactly what the writer is thinking. The use of 'etc.' should be restricted and used only when it is absolutely needed.

5. Using the suffix '–ish' to many nouns has become a common practice. Formal language does not accept it.

Wrong: Mrs. Gupta is fortyish and rich.
Right: Mrs. Gupta is in her forties and is rich.

34

QUESTIONS AND ANSWERS

This section deals with questions and answers. We have many doubts in our minds. We see many doubtful usages / words in papers, magazines, and we also hear many words / phrases that create doubts in our minds—all are presented in a question and answer format. The reader is expected to refer to more and more books and satisfy his curiosity. Some answers and explanations given here are disputable, whereas others are acceptable. Some of the explanations may be too much for a beginner and he can take it up later.

The reasons for this Q and A format are:

1. Reader-friendly approach or concept.
2. To break the monotony of 'para after para' type of presentation.
3. To include various topics under one section.
4. Have something to offer, to beginners, experts.
5. To make the book novel, fresh, interesting, different and unusual.

1. What is the difference between 'choose' and 'pick'?

   Although many people tend to use the words synonymously it should be kept in mind that there is a distinction between the two words. Do you 'choose' your life partner, or do you 'pick' one? Normally people choose their significant other. Choose suggests that you have opted for the individual after aivina the matter serious thought. You have weighed the pros and cons of an issue in this case marrying a person – and have arrived at a considered decision. It is voluntary. Pick also means selection but in this case there you have opted for something in a very casual manner – there may not be any decision making or discrimination involved. When you go to a supermarket and see several cans or packets of the same product you normally don't take too much time thinking about whether to buy a packet or a can. Since the same company has made them, you pick the can / packet that is nearest to you. Most of us do not select our life partner in this casual manner. Similarly we choose a present keeping in mind a person's likes and dislikes. If we pick a present what we are doing is buying something in a casual manner. We don't keep in mind the individual's likes and dislikes; it suggest that we buy the first thing we see in the shop.

Choose	Pick
Used in more 'serious' parlance.	No serious thinking involved.
Involves decision making/ discrimination.	Used in a 'casual' content.
Means 'selection'.	Means 'selection'.
Examples	*Example*
People choose their life partner (not pick).	*People pick up grocery in the super market.*

2. What is the meaning of *'too close to call'*? This is an expression we hear very often from reporters during elections and from commentators during one-day matches when you say that a game is too close to call. What you mean is that it is evenly poised, and it is almost impossible to predict which team will emerge, the winner when used during election what it implies is that the two candidates are running neck and neck and therefore predicting the ultimate winner is not possible right then. *The counting is going on, the result is too close to call.*

3. Is it all right to say 'Wish you a happy new year 2005'?
   No, it is not. When you want to greet someone on the New Year's day, you say, "Happy New Year" or "Wish You a Happy New Year". Do not include the actual year – in this case 2005 – along with the greeting if you want to give importance to the year. Some do say "Happy 2005" or "Wish you a happy 2005".
4. What is the difference between 'disposed of' and 'disposed off' ?
   When you get rid of someone or something you say 'disposed of', not 'disposed off'. 'Disposed off' is incorrect.

Example

I want to know how the murderer disposed of the bodies.

In informal contexts when you say that you disposed of someone, what you mean is that you killed him. Perhaps you hired someone to do the killing.

Example

The don asked his hit man to dispose of his former accountant.

5. What is the difference between 'blue collar worker' and 'pink collar worker'?
   A *'blue collar worker* works' in an industry and is always involved in manual labour. You will find this individual in factories sweating it out on the shop floor. You won't find him sitting behind a huge desk in an office. Nowadays the term can be applied to both men and women. 'Pink collar workers', on the other hand, are always women. Low-paid jobs are available in offices and restaurants are usually referred to as 'Pink collar jobs'. 'White collar' is an adjective (of worker or work) – non-manual 'clerical'.
6. What is the difference between 'abbreviations' and 'acronyms'?

Abbreviation is the shortened form of words.

Example

Bachelor of arts is abbreviated as BA.

Dr., Mr., Ph.D, U.A.E, U.K, U.S. are all similar abbreviations of bigger words.

Similarly,

'e.g.'	for exampligratia
etc.	for etcetera
p.s.	post script
p.t.o.	please turn over
Pub.	public house
m.p.h / km.p.h	mles per hour / kilometres per hour
LIC	Life Insurance Corporation of India
co.	company
IAS	Indian Adminstrative Service
CM	Chief Minister
St.	Saint / street
Ltd.	Limited
TV	television

Abbreviations have become an important part of spoken and written English today.

An 'acronym' is a word formed from the initial letters of other words.

Example

North Atlantic Treaty Organization –NATO (N-A-T-O – the initial letters).

Such new words formed from the initial letters of others and easy to pronounce are called Acronyms.

Examples

SPIC

NASA

CAT

TOEFL

Maths (Mathematics)

Xmas (Christmas)

GATT (General Agreement on Tariffs and Trade)

7. What is the meaning of the word 'willy-nilly'. How is this word used?

   'Willy-nilly' means 'whether one desires it or not'. It is used as an adverb.

Example

Willy-nilly you have to be in the office till 8 p.m.

In English you have many such words which have two words with a slight difference in their sound.

(a) Dilly-dally: used as a verb; colloquially it means to dawble; waste time by indecision.

(b) Tittle-tattle: used as a verb and as a noun. As noun it means gossip, rumour, hearsay, talk; as a verb it only means gossip.

(c) Topsy-turvy: used as an adverb and adjecive as an adverb it means upside down; In or into great disorder as an adjective it also means chaotic, messy, untidy.

(d) 'Hanky-panky': used as a noun. It means to cheat someone cleverly by trick; craftly deceitful act.

(e) ZigZag: means line or course turning right and left alternatively at sharp angles. Used as a noun.

This word also finds use as:

Verb	Adverb	Adjective
Zigzagged	as or in a zigzag	

8. Can the verb 'discuss' be used with the preposition 'about'?

Example

The officers discussed the problems of tsunami victims.

Is this sentence correct?

The verb 'discuss' is used along with the preposition 'with'. When 'discuss' and 'with' are used together to make 'discuss' function as a verb, there is always a person who comes after the word 'with'.

Example

a. Ramu discussed it with me.
b. The Prime Minister discussed the issues with his ministers.
c. Discuss something with somebody.

When the verb 'discuss' becomes the noun discussion, 'about' and 'on' join it.

Example

a. We had a fruitful discussion about welfare schemes.
b. There was a discussion about/on money.
c. She discussed the problems, (here 'discuss' is a verb).
d. Her discussion about/on politics was interesting (here discussion is a noun.
e. The officers had a discussion about the problems of tsunami victims.

9. What does the ZIP in Zip code stand for?

   The ZIP in zip code stands for 'Zoning Improvements Plan'.

10. How should 'ough' be pronounced?

    'Ough' can be pronounced in eight different ways. The following sentence contains them all. 'A rough-coated, *dough*-faced ploughman strode through the streets of *Scarborough, coughing* and *hiccoughing* thoughtfully.

11. What do these words mean?

    Epigram, epilogue, epitome, epitaph, epithalamium

    epigram – Short witty sayings.

    Epilogue – Short concluding section.

    Epitome – Person or thing embodying a quality etc.

    Epitaph – Words in memory of a dead person, especially, on a tomb.

Epithalamium – A poem written to celebrate a wedding.

12. What is the origin of the term 'slap-stick comedy'?

A punch and Judy show always includes a lot of puppets bashing other puppets around the head with a stick. The stick is usually a slap stick, a stick with two small paddles on the end of it, or a stick which is carefully sewn lengthwise at one or both ends to make a loud noise when it hits a wooden head. This was a favourite device of the Italian Commedia dell' Art and this is the origin of the term 'slap stick comedy'.

Example

That movie has nothing but slap-stick comedy to offer.

13. What is the meaning, origin and the context of use of the word 'paparazzi'?

'Paparazzi', plural of 'paparazzo', comes from the name of a character in Fellini's *La dolce Vita*. In the movie, Paparazzo was a photographer who would go to great lengths to take pictures of American movie stars.

Examples

a. The paparazzi is to be blamed for princess Diana's death.
b. The actors and actresses rushed into the theatre to avoid the paparazzi.
c. The pop singer came in a different get up to avoid the paparazzi.

14. What is the origin of these words?

a. Algorithm – *Al khowarizmi* (Arab mathematics)
b. August – *Augustus Caesar*
c. Bougainvillea – *Louis Antoine de Bougainville* (French explorer)
d. Casanova – *Giovanni Jacopo Casanova de Seingalt* (Italian adventurer)
e. Jaccuzi – *Roy Jacuzzi and Candido Jacuzzi* (American inventors)
f. Side-burns – *Gen. Ambrose Everett Burnside* (union soldier).

g. Levis – *Levi Strauss* Bavarian immigrant to the USA and clothing merchant.

All these words have the same type of origin—they are all names that became words.

15. 'Giving, given' both are participles. There are a lot of doubts in their meaning and correct usage. How should one use these participles without errors?

Give, gave, given, giving – all these are various forms of the verb 'give' (cause to receive or have; provide with)

Given – past participle

Giving – present participle

Both 'given' and 'giving' usually follow the verb 'be'.

Be + given ('be given' refers to something that has been given).

Be + giving ('be giving' refers to something that is in the process of being given).

Examples

a. They are given protection.
b. He was given punishment.
c. The children will be given prizes.
d. Food and clothes were given to the tsunami-affected people.
e. Medicine and injections are given to prevent epidemic.

'Be given' is always in the passive voice.

In perfect tense given joins with 'have / has / had'.

Examples

a. They have given their support.
b. The teacher had given them exercise.

Be + giving

Examples

a. The cows are giving milk.
b. He was giving instruction.

c. The people have been giving shelter to the poor.

'Giving' gives the meaning as a gerund (subject) and verbal noun (object).

Examples

a. Giving is a pleasure.

b. He enjoys giving everything to others.

16. 'Little, a little': Do these words have any differences? How are these words used? Yes! These two words have differences in meanings. When we use the word 'little' it implies a negative thought, that is; no /nil.

Example: We have little water.

This implies "We don't have any water."

Example: We have a little water.

This implies "We have some (though the amount is less) water.

Little implies nil or no. 'A little' implies less.

Similarly when we use the words 'few' and 'a few' the meanings are as above.

Few implies not many.

Example: She has *few* friends.

This means she has no friends at all.

Example: She has a few friends.

This means she has not many (less in number) friends.

'Few' and 'a few' are used with countable nouns.

'Little' and 'a little' are used with uncountable nouns.

'Few friends', 'a few friends'.

The number of friends can be counted, hence a countable noun.

Little milk, a little milk: milk cannot be counted as one, two, three. Hence it is an uncountable noun.

We see that when the article 'a' is added to 'few' or 'little' it brings about a total change in the meaning.

While using articles 'a', 'an', one must be careful. Few / little gives a negative meaning, a few/a little imply a positive meaning.

This point must be kept in mind while adding articles to such words.

17. In literary terms what do the words Didactic, Diction, Horatian Satire, Soliloquy mean?

One often comes across such terms both in books and in competitive exams. The following explantions are given below.

1. **Didactic** – A term used to describe works of literature that aim to teach some moral, religious, political or practical lesson, although didactic elements are often found in artistically pleasing works. The term *didactic* usually refers to literature in which the message is more important than the critic finds, "overly didactic", that is, heavy-handed in its delivery of a lesson. Examples of didactic literature include John Bunyan's *Pilgrim's Progress*.
2. **Diction** – An author's choice of words. Since words have specific meanings and since one's choice of words can affect feelings, a writer's choice of words can have great impact in a literary work.
3. **Horatian Satire** – In general, a gentler, more good-humoured and sympathetic kind of satire, somewhat tolerant of human folly even while laughing at it. Named after Horace whose satire epitomised it. Horatian satire tends to ridicule human folly in general or by type rather than attack specific persons.
4. **Soliloquy** – In drama, a moment when a character is alone and speaks his or her thoughts aloud.

18. What do the words 'white hope', 'white lie' and 'white elephant' mean?

White hope refers to a person expected to achieve much. *White lie* means a harmless lie; *white elephant* refers to a useless possession.

19. What does the phrase 'cuts a sorry figure' mean? How should one use such a phrase?

    'Cuts a sorry figure' is an idiom. It is established by usage and not immediately from the words used. It is a form of expression peculiar to a language (here it is English).

    It means to get into a situation of ridicule, to become the subject of humour; becoming pathetic, pitiful due to the situation or in the situation.

Example

She could not answer the question of the lawyer. She cut a sorry figure.

'Cut a fine figure' (means to be in an admirable / enviable position).

'Cut a poor figure' (means to be in a piliable, non-enviable position).

Idioms are to be used keeping in mind the meaning and the context.

a. 'To eat ones' words means to take back / go back on spoken words, facts or data.
b. 'To make both ends meet' means to spend within means.
c. 'To turn a new leaf' means to start a new life.
d. 'To turn a deaf ear' means deliberately not listening to instructions, not doing things.
e. 'By hook or by crook' means by fair or unfair means.
f. 'From hand to mouth' means difficult poverty-driven life.
g. 'At sixes and sevens' means a confused state of affairs.
h. 'Out of date' means obsolete, not in use.
i. 'Up to date' means very new, recent.
j. 'By and by' means slowly, step by step.
k. 'By the by' means in between.

Examples

a. He works hard but cannot make both ends meet.

b. He earned fame by and by.
c. They wanted this contract by hook or by crook.

20. What are the common errors in using the word 'even'?

'Even' has many meanings in English. 'Even numbers' refers to numbers such as 2,4,6,8... (odd numbers refers to 1,3,5,7,...). 'Even ground' means ground which is smooth, without any elevations / depressions; smooth, regular surface without any irregularities; uniform level / plane.

'Even breathing' means regular, breathing; calm, rhythmical, steady, unbroken, unvarying.

'Even song' refers to an evening song.

'Even' is also used in comparing things or for emphasis.

Example

It was cold yesterday but it is even colder today.

Even though is used as:

a. an adjective – meaning level, smooth, uniform, calm, equal.
b. a verb – make or become even
c. an adverb – to compare things

When we use 'if' or 'though' with 'even ' ('even if' 'even though'), we get the meaning as shown in the examples.

Examples

a. She won't leave her TV set even though her father is waiting for his supper.
b. Even if Ramu comes, Gopal cannot teach him

'Even now', 'even then' bring about the meanings as follows.

Examples

a. He explained everything but even then she would not believe him.
b. Even now at the age of sixty Gayatri Devi looks beautiful.

Even as, even with, even out, even up, even handed, break even – are other terms in which even is used.

21. What is the difference between 'had better', 'would rather'?

'Had better' is used to mean: doing something according to rule books, conscience; it implies something which has to be done (compulsorily).

'Had better' is used in prose, speech, dialogue. This is used to emphasize what one has to do to avoid difficulties and faults.

Examples

a. You'd better leave now before you get into any trouble.
b. You'd better mind your business.
c. You'd better not say that.

We see that 'had better' is followed by the present form of the main verb like leave, mind, say. One must remember that 'you'd' is the short form of 'you had'.

'Would rather' is used to mean: doing something out of choice, voluntarily. In some context 'had rather' is also used.

Examples

a. I'd rather take vegetarian food than non-vegetarian.
b. She'd rather study English than maths.
c. "Will you join us in a game of cards?" askedPeter. "Thank you, but I'd rather not," said Charles.

Here *I'd rather, she'd rather* are short forms of *I would rather; she would rather*.

22. 'Provided, providing' – how should these be used?

These words are used in sentences as 'provided that' and 'providing that'. Both these mean 'if' (on condition that, supposing that).

Examples

a. Provided that there is no opposition I will do the assignment.
b. She will go provided that you pay her money.
c. The people will work provided that the leaders too work.

23. To, by, in, into, with, within, without, from, of, off, at. How should one use these prepositions?

One should keep in mind that prepositions are used in different contexts and the meanings also change according to the context.

In: place and time both are involved while using 'in'.

Example

a. She is *in* the garden (place).
b. She will come *in* an hour (time).

Into: implies to the inside of, to a point within, to a particular state.

Example

a. Thieves broke *into* his house.
b. Throw the wastepaper *into* the fire.
c. The snow changed *into* water.

With: implies in the company of, among, having.

Example

a. He went to the church *with* his children.
b. The boy wore a shirt *with* two pockets.

Within: implies inside, not beyond the limit or scope of.

Example

a. Stay *within* my reach.
b. live *within* your income.

Without not having, in the absence of.

Example

a. There is no smoke *without* fire.
b. I can't go *without* tickets.

From: having as the starting point, source or cause.

Example:

a. A cool wind blew *from* the north.
b. The river comes *from* the mountain.
c. The prisoner escaped *from* the jail.

Of : belonging to, from.

Off: away, out of position.

Example

a. She is proud of her beauty.
b. He is cured of his sickness.
c. The tulips of our garden are beautiful.
d. He fell off a tree.
e. The railway station is five kilometres off.
f. The bus terminus is two kilometres off.

At: having as position, time of day. 'At' denotes both time and place like 'in'.

Example

a. He is at his office (place).
b. I will meet you in the afternoon.
c. I will meet you at 3 p.m.

By: mainly implies 'near, beside, through the agency, means of'.

Example

a. The college is by the court.
b. He went to England by flight.
c. The work is done by them.

To: towards, as compared with 'in respect of, as far as' etc.

Example

a. They went to school.
b. She was reading with her legs stretched out to the fire.

From the above examples one can understand the various contexts of using prepositions.

24. What do the noun 'toll' and the verb 'toll' mean?

The noun 'toll' means tax paid for the use of a public road, etc. It also means loss / damage by a disaster (e.g., death toll). The verb 'toll' means ring with slow strokes, especially to mark a death.

25. What do the words 'bachelor', 'spinster' and 'confirmed bachelor' mean?

'Bachelor' means an unmarried man; 'spinster' means a woman who remains single after the usual age of marrying; 'confirmed bachelor' means a single man who has decided never to marry.

Examples

a. He is a bachelor.
b. She is a spinster.
c. Ramu is thirty-five years old and is a confirmed bachelor.

26. What are 'litotes'? An ironical understatement in which an affirmative is expressed by the negative of the contrary.

27. How are 'by' and 'by law' used?

The Danes introduced the 'by' into English. It stands for village; so 'by law' means 'village' or local law (law also has a Danish derivation).

What is a 'slang'?

28. Words or phrases or particular meanings of these are used very informally for vividness or novelty. The language of Americans has become a slang. A survey in 1997 showed how the classical language of 1492 (the year America was discovered) had changed to a slang in 405 years. Certain testimonies to this conclusion are as below:

Awol – acronym for 'absent without leave'.

Blow smoke – to boast, brag or exaggerate.

Dance on air – to die by hanging.

Eagle freak – a conservationist or enviromentalist.

Head shrinker – psychiatrist or psychologist (shrink).

Lunch hooks – the hands.

Nose job – plastic surgery to beautify a nose.

On a raft – on a slice of toast.

Rib tickles – something amusing.

Up chuck – to vomit.

Wheeze – an old joke.

Yellow belly – a coward.

29. What does the word 'pugilist' mean?

A pugilist is a boxer.

Example

Perhaps the world's most popular pugilist is Mohammad Ali.

'Pugilist' and 'punctuation' come from the same root, a Latin word meaning 'to sting'.

30. What does the word 'goof ball' mean?

'Goof ball' means a stupid person but it is also an American slang for drug in tablet form, especially barbiturate (any group of sedative drug).

31. What does the term 'A bread and butter letter' mean?

It refers to a letter thanking a host / hostess for his / her hospitality.

32. What does the word 'bravura' mean?

The word means brilliant style or technique usually in musical performances.

Example

It was a bravura performance all right!! (shout of approval at an actor's performance).

It must have come from brave because bravura performance will make one cry 'Bravo!'.

33. Talking about gender what is a count's wife called? What is an earls wife called?

A count's wife is called a countess. An earl's wife is also called, countess.

34. What do the terms 'bilinigual' and 'polyglot' mean?

'Bilingual' means two languages.

Example

Maniratnam, the famous director, is making a bilingual movie.

'Polyglot' refers to many languages. A person who knows many languages is called a polyglot.

Example

The news reader in BBC is a polyglot.

35. How is the word 'crack' used in a different context?

a) *'Crack down'* or someone or something: Impose more severe treatment or restrictions on something / someone.

Example

'Cracking down' on drug dealers.

The noun form is crack down.

Example

A crack down on tax evasion.

b) *'Crack up' to be* something (idiom, informal, usually negative) reputed to be something.

Example

She is not such a good dancer as she is cracked up to be.

c) 'The *crack of dawn*' – (idiom, informal) very early in the morning.

Example

Do you usually get up at the crack of dawn?

d) 'Crack up' (informal)— lose one's health, mentally or physically.

Example: he will crack up if he goes on like this.

e) Paper over the cracks (idiom) – hide a disagreement, fault or difficulty especially quickly or imperfectly.

Example

The new measures introduced to crack down on eve teasers are simply papering over the cracks.

36. What is the full form of the acronym WYSIWYG? What you see is what you get.

37. What is the origin of the expression "shoot from the hip"?

It means to act impulsively or impetuously. This refers to the act of firing a hand gun at a person or an object.

38. What do the word 'billboards' mean?

Billboards is the name given to hoardings in the USA.

39. What is the difference between 'extradition' and 'deportation'?

'Extradition' means the removal of a criminal to the country where he has fled to avoid prosecution or prison. 'Deportation' is expulsion of an alien whose presence is deemed inconsistent with public welfare.

40. What does the phrase 'to mind ones p's and q's' mean?

It means to be careful of one's behaviour.

41. How is the word 'foot' used in English?

i. *'Foot work',* – ability to react quickly to sudden danger, new opportunities, etc. (figuratively).

ii. 'Foot slog' – walk for a long distance and so become tired.

iii. 'Footloose' – without personal responsibilities or commitments, free to act as one pleases.

iv. 'Foothold' – secure position in a business profession, etc. from which further progresses may be made.

v. 'Foot fault' – act of breaking the rules in tennis by placing your feet inside the backline when serving the ball.

42. What does the following proverb mean: 'What is sauce for the goose is sauce for the gander'?

This means that what applies to one person must apply to another in similar circumstances.

43. What is a 'car boot sale'? Is this term relevant in India?

It is a kind of outdoor sale. You sell unwanted possession dumped in the boot (compartment for luggage) of your car. The US term for 'carboot sale' is 'garage sale'.

44. Politicians often use the Latin phrase 'vox populi'. What does it mean? It means the voice of the people.

45. What does the word 'yuppies' mean? How it is used?

The word 'yuppies' was born in New York, in Nov 21, 1984. The word comprises the first letters of young urban professional plus some extra fitting. It was the craze in the 1980s. Especially in Britain, yuppies were given the admirable status of the upwardly mobile youth. When someone tries to move up in the moneyed class using his respectable social status, background and contacts we call it social climbing. But if he makes it regardless of the social background and by virtue of his own cleverness and hard work we call that person upwardly mobile. So yuppies was not a bad word, at least to begin with. It referred to youngsters who pounced on every money-making opportunity with an aggressiveness that was encouraged by modern marketing experts. Now the word brings into your mind the kind of boys and girls with long hair, sleeveless T-shirt, faded jeans, smoking drugs, etc. Godfrey Howard says, " After the stock market crash in autumn 1987, Yuppies ran out of steam. The recession of the early 1990s finished it off, as thousands of young executives working for financial company's were made redundant. Although still heard, yuppie sounds like one of yesterday's words and there is little point in using it any more."

A 'buppie' is a black urban professional who is upwardly mobile.

Guppie – green yuppie (an envoirmental yuppie).

Juppie – Japanese yuppie.

Puppie – Pregnant yuppie (also Punjabi yuppie in India).

Yupskies – Russian yuppie (so called as many Russian words end with sky or ski).

All these above-mentioned yuppie clones did not survive much.

46. Does the word 'Elders' have any other meaning?

Apart from meaning older, Elders also has another

meaning; irrespective of their ages members of the Rajya Sabha are known as Elders.

47. Colloquially who is a Fuss Pot?

A person given to excessive concern over a trivial issue.

48. What do the following words mean? Can they be used?

'Grey area' – any uncertain, ill-defined policy, attitude ruling, etc.

'Nightmare scenario' – any situation with a possible outcome that would lead to much more serious problems. The term was used when in 1991 the Gulf was struck and Saddam Hussain was forced to withdraw from Kuwait.

'Dream ticket' – originally the term meant the ideal leadership combination that offers a political party a good opportunity to win the next election. A 'dream ticket' is usually a political term. The term can be used non-politically too; to mean any promising combination and at least it can be pointed out that it is the opposite of a nightmare scenario.

49. What are the important points one needs to remember while using singular and plural nouns?

a. There are some nouns in the English language having the singular and plural alike. That is to say there is no separate plural form. Such nouns are usually used only in singular form.

Example

series, species, politics, offspring, fish, deer.

b. There are some nouns which denote number, measure and these do not change form in the plural when they are used after numerals.

Example

hundreds, thousand, dozen, score.

c. Some nouns are used in singular only.

Example

fruit, poetry, hair, furniture.

iv. Some nouns are plural in form but singular in use .

Example

economics, physics, mechanics, measles.

v. Some nouns are singular in form but plural in use.

Example

folk, police, public.

vi. Some nouns are used in plural only.

Example

pincers, scissors, spectacles, shorts, intestines, savings, earnings, etc.

50. What is a personal pronoun?

The personal pronouns – mine, ours, hers, theirs, yours are also called possessive pronouns. They are not followed by nouns.

Example:

a. This bat is *mine*.
b. My son and *yours* are close friends.
c. This book *is his* or This is *his* book.
d. The daughter of *yours* is very intelligent.

The basic rules are: possessive pronouns are used when the noun is not expressed; when a verb comes between the noun and the possessive pronoun.

51. What are the adjectives used only in the positive and the superlative degrees?

Adjectives like top, northern, southern, eastern, western are positives and their superlative counterparts are topmost, northernmost, southernmost, easternmost, westernmost.

52. What is the difference between the following pairs of words which are so similar in meaning?

a. Amiable, Amicable

'Amiable' means pleasant and good tempered; easy and

pleasant to talk to.

'Amicable' means done in a friendly way.

Examples

i. Sita is an amiable girl.

ii. The landlord and the tenant reached an amicable settlement.

b. Character, Reputation

'Character' means mental or moral qualities that make a person, group, nations, etc. different from others.

'Reputation' signifies what is generally said or believed about the abilities, qualities, etc., of somebody or something.

Examples

i. Gopal is a man of strong character.

ii. Vikram Seth has a reputation as a good author.

c. Custom, Habit

'Custom' means usual and generally accepted and long established way of behaving or doing things among members of a social group.

'Habit' means something that a person does often, almost without thinking, specially something that is hard to stop doing.

('Ritual' is a series of actions used in a religious ceremony.)

Example

i. Social customs and traditions vary in different families.

ii. Suresh has a nervous habit of biting his nails.

iii. Arun does not believe in religious rituals.

53. What are the appropriate female genders for:

tailor, tutor, monk, fiance, waiter, heir, mayor?

1. Tailor - Tailoress
2. Tutor - Tutoress

3. Monk - Nun
4. Fiance - Fiancee
5. Waiter - Waitress
6. Heir - Heiress
7. Mayor - Mayoress

What are the corresponding male genders?

1. Hen-sparrow - Cock-sparrow
2. She-goat (Nanny-goat) - He-goat (Billy-goat)
3. Mare - Horse
4. Duck - Drake
5. Heifer - Bullock
6. Cow-calf - Bull-calf
7. Bee - Drone

54. What are the corresponding plurals for the following singulars?

1. Speech - Speeches
2. Loss - Losses
3. Monarch - Monarchs
4. Fly - Flies
5. Study - Studies
6. Way - Ways
7. Storey - Storeys
8. Volcano - Volcanoes
9. Photo - Photos
10. Halo - Halos or Haloes
11. Cuckoo - Cuckoos
12. Knife - Knives

55. What are the corresponding singulars for the plurals given below?

Chiefs - Chief

Proofs - Proof

Selves	-	Self
Scarfs (Scarves)	-	Scarf
Feet	-	Foot
Teeth	-	Tooth
Men	-	Man
Women	-	Woman
Geese	-	Goose

56. What are the corresponding plurals for the singulars

1.	German	-	Germans
2.	Ox	-	Oxen
3.	School Book	-	School books
4.	Boyfriend	-	Boyfriends
5.	Lord-justice	-	Lords-justice
6.	Looker-on	-	Lookers-on
7.	Daughter-in-law	-	Daughters-in-law
8.	Mouse	-	Mice
9.	Mouthful	-	Mouthfuls
10.	B.A.	-	B.A.'s
11.	Sheep	-	Sheep
12.	Fish	-	Fish (or fishes)

57. What is the meaning of the expression 'a hatchet job'?

Americans usually refer to an axe as a hatchet. When you say that some reporter did a hatchet job on you what you mean is that he criticised you severely in the media. The criticism is usually unfair criticism.

Example: The news channels did a hatchet job on the prime minister's visit to the earthquake-hit areas.

58. What does the expression 'to open a can of worms' mean?

When someone says that he is going to do something and you tell him not to open a can of worms, you are warning him not to do anything. You are suggesting that the situation is so complicated that if he starts dealing with the problem he will only succeed in creating more problems for himself. By trying to solve the problem he will be creating more problems.

Example: Introducing my best friend's brother to my parents has opened up a big can of worms.

59. What does 'sail into someone' syntax mean?

One of the meanings of 'sail into someone' is to attack or scold someone. It is an expression usually used in an informal context.

Example: The young bride sailed into her husband for bringing his friends unannounced.

60. What are the rules for using the words *can, could, do, have*?

'Can' is a modal auxi'iary verb. The negative of *can* is *cannot*, and the contracted form is *can't*.

'Can' is used to indicate ability, acquired knowledge or kill, permission, request, possibility.

Examples

i. She can solve this problem.
ii. She can sing well.
iii. Can I read your report?
iv. Can you tell me the time?
v. Can the news be true?

'Cannot' is used to mean 'be unable to', 'be incapable of'.

Examples

She cannot walk very fast.

He cannot swim.

He cannot play football.

'Could' is a modal auxiliary verb. The negative form of 'could' is *could not* and the contracted form is *couldn't*.

'Could' is used to indicate ability in the past, permission, request, result, suggestions.

Examples

i. Five years ago, I could walk three miles at a stretch.
ii. Could I accompany her to school?
iii. Could you do me a small favour?
iv. She is so happy that she could jump with joy.
v. You could always try her mobile number.

'Do' is a principal auxiliary verb. The negative of do is *do not* and the contracted form is *don't*.

'Do' is used to form the negative of main verbs, to form questions, to give emphasis to the main verb when there is no other auxiliary.

Examples

i. I do not play cricket.
ii. Do you speak Hindi?
iii. Do come and see me next week.

Do is also used to make comparisons.

Examples

Arun drives faster than I do.

'Have' – principal auxiliary verb; the negative form is *have not*; the contracted form is *haven't*.

Examples

i. Have you seen him?
ii. I have finished my report (present perfect).
iii. I have been singing for two hours (present perfect).
iv. He will have become a doctor by this time – next year (future perfect).
v. I shall have written two books by the end of this year (future perfect).

'Have' is also used as a full verb to denote:

i. Possess or own something.
ii. Experience or feel something.
iii. .eceive something.

iv. Produce.
v. Indicating a relationship.

Examples

i. I have an estate in Ooty.
ii. I have no doubt that Bala is dishonest.
iii. How often do you have French lessons in a week?
iv. This medicine will have a good effect on his headache.
v. I have two daughters and one son.

61. What do the following words mean?

omnipotent, iconoclast, verbatim, ambidextrous, verbose.

'Omnipotent' means all powerful.

Examples

God is omnipotent (note omnipotent – present everywhere; omniscient – knows everything).

'Verbatim' – To produce a passage word for word in exactly the same words.

Examples

The manager repeated the instruction of his boss verbatim.

Ambidextrous – the man who can use either hand with ease.

Examples

Among *Pancha Pandavas* Arjuna was ambidextrous.

'Verbose' – a style that is full of words; using more words than are needed.

Examples

Our teacher criticised Arun's verbose essay.

'Iconoclast' – breaker of images.

In a deeper sense iconoclast means a person who attacks cherished belief.

Examples

Suresh is an agnostic and also an iconoclast.

62. How should one use 'may' and 'might' correctly?

Both 'may' and 'might' are modal auxiliary verbs. Their negative forms are *may not* and *might not*. Their contracted forms are *mayn't* and *mightn't*. We will see their context.

May is used to indicate a request, possibility and uncertainty.

Examples

i. May I know where Gopal lives?
ii. This bag may be Aruna's.
iii. She may have come by bus.

'Might' is used to indicate possibility, request, polite suggestions.

Examples

i. That might be our answer sheets.
ii. She asked me if she might borrow a pencil.
iii. You might like to comment on his latest report.

63. What are the malapropisms in the following sentences.

Wrong

i. She is not a woman of principals.
ii. John asked Mary for ten scents.
iii. Govinda is a mare clerk in AG office.
iv. Gita asked Sita for some floor to make chappatis.
v. Gujral has many diary farms.
vi. He preys to God every night.
vii. Shiva rushed from Singapore to perform his father's last rights.

Right

i. She is not a woman of principles.
ii. John asked Mary for ten cents.
iii. Govinda is a mere clerk in the AG office.
iv. Gita asked Sita for some flour to make chappatis.

v. Gujral has many dairy farms.
vi. He prays to God every night.
vii. Shiva rushed from Singapore to perform his father's last rites.

64. What does the word 'Accordion management' mean? Where in this word used?

Business buzz words have become highly visible, value laden symbols of the revolution, moving management in new directions. Accordion management is one of the new words in the growing *vocabulary of business*. It means the ability to grow or shrink a work force quickly and at will by hiring or releasing temporary workforce.

65. Does the words 'Mural' and 'Fresco' mean the same?

A 'mural' is a painting executed directly on a wall, while a 'fresco' is a painting done in water colour on a wall or ceiling while the plaster is still wet. Therefore, these two words don't exactly mean the same.

66. What does the word vegetarian denote? What is its origin?

The word 'vegetarian' means a person who eats no meat or fish. It originated from a Latin word *vegetus* meaning 'healthy, lively'.

67. What is the meaning of the term 'bakers dozen'?

Bakers dozen is thirteen. In the sixteenth century, English bakers were fined heavily for selling short-weighted loaves of bread, and to guard against this it became customary for them to throw in an extra loaf called the 'in bread' whenever a retailer purchased a dozen. Thus a dozen plus one became known as 'baker's dozen'.

68. Check the malapropisms in the following sentences

Wrong

1. Please do rite a letter to your daddy.
2. The cruel landlords steel the life and labour of workers.
3. The ship reached the heaven.
4. The law must take its own coarse.

5. Shah Rukh Khan's roll in that movie is bad.

Right

1. Please do write a letter to your daddy.
2. The cruel landlords steal the life and labour of workers.
3. The ship reached the haven.
4. The law must take its own course.
5. Shah Rukh Khan's role in that movie is bad.

69. How should the verbs *shall, should, will, would* be used?

'Shall' and 'should' are modal auxiliary verbs.

Their negative counterparts are *shall not, should not*.

The contracted forms are *shan't* and *shouldn't*.

Shall is used to indicate future predictions and suggestions.

Examples

i. I shall see Ramu next week.
ii. I shall be twenty-six next month.
iii. Shall I post this card for you?
iv. Shall I sit down here?

'Should' is used to indicate obligation, advice.

Examples

i. We should obey the laws.
ii. We should respect our parents.
iii. You should not smoke here.
iv. You should work hard.

'Will' and 'would' are modal auxiliary verbs. Their respective negatives are *will not* and *would not*. Their contracted forms are *won't* and *wouldn't*.

'Will' is used to indicate polite invitation, promise.

Examples

i. Will you attend my tea party?
ii. Will you have a cup of coffee?
iii. I will help you every week.
iv. I will pay back your loan next week.

'Would' is used to describe the consequence of an imagined event, a hypothetical action, etc.

Examples

i. I would establish an old age home if I won a lottery.

ii. If I had seen the contest advertisement, I would have

iii. participated in it.

iv. Would I be able to help her?

70. What do the words mean toxin, tocsin?

Toxin – Poisonous substance especially formed in the body.

Tocsin – An alarm signal or bell.

71. How should the verbs *must, need, dare* and *ought* be used?

All the fours are modal auxiliary verbs. Their respective negatives and contracted forms are *must not, mustn't, need not, needn't, dare not, daren't, ought not, oughtn't.*

1. 'Must' is used to indicate probability, obligation, insistence, necessity, etc.

Examples

You must hurry. You are late for school (note the necessity).

2. 'Need to' has similar uses. It indicates obligation; it indicates actions which have been unnecessary.

Examples

You need not have bought it (see the indication of an action which is unnecessary).

'Need' is also used as a noun.

3. 'Dare' usually indicates 'have sufficient courage or impudence to do something'.

Examples

How dare he say such horrible things about me?

4. 'Ought', indicates obligation, advice, recommendation, etc.

Example

You ought to apologise to her.

72. What does the verb 'truckle' mean?

'Truckle' means to yield or bend to the will of another; to act in a subservient manner.

Example

It is fatal to truckle to what one conceives to be popular taste.

73. How does one use the verb 'cloy'? What does it mean?

'Cloy' means to cause disgust because of our indulgence, especially of something rich and sweet.

Example

Her sickeningly sweet personality is cloying which makes everyone nauseous.

74. What is the meaning of monarchy, democracy, anarchy, dictatorship?

It is often seen that these terms are used in the wrong contexts.

One is interchanged for another as they sound similar and have to do with the same subject.

'Monarchy' is rule by a king.

'Democracy' is rule of the people.

'Anarchy' is state of having no government.

'Dictatorship' is rule by a tyrant.

Here it will be interesting to discuss a group of similar confusing words: aristocracy, autocracy, bureaucracy.

Aristocracy – refers to hereditary upper class.

Autocracy – despotism (a kind of dictatorship type of authority).

Bureaucracy – government by unelected officials' excessive administration.

75. If 'feline' is catlike what does 'anserine' like?

'Anserine' is goose-like.

76. What does the word 'quadragenerians' refer to?

It refers to the 40 to 49-year olds.

77. What does 'vulpine' mean?

It means of or resembling a fox; crafty, cunning or sly.

Example

That vulpine salesperson would sell swamp land to his own mother if he had the choice.

78. What do 'faux pas', 'cagnoscenti' mean? How are they used?

Faux pas – embarrassing mistake that one makes in a social context.

Example: She felt embarrassed at the faux pas she had made.

Cognoscenti – connoisseur.

Example

For Amrita's painting exhibition, the city's cognoscenti was present in full measure.

79. What do retinue, lugubrious, obdurate mean?

Retinue – attendant accompanying an important person.

Example: The prime minister and his retinue reached the meeting safely.

Lugubrious — dismal, forlorn, gloomy, miserable.

Example: The condition of flood victims is Lugubrious.

Obdurate – stubborn.

Example: Kavita is headstrong and obdurate by nature.

80. How should the speech be corrected in the following sentences?

Wrong

1. He *said to* her who she was.
2. I said, Aruna *may* come.
3. He said to me that he *purchased* a cycle.

4. Geeta said that she will meet me now.
5. He said that God was everywhere.
6. I said that I am reading a book.
7. He told farewell to his friend.
8. I said to Sita if she will buy a new kurta.
9. Gopal asked me whether I play basketball.
10. Mohan said to Sohan where he lives.

Right

1. He asked her who she was.
2. I said, Aruna might come.
3. He said to me that he had purchased a cycle.
4. Geeta said that she would meet me now.
5. He said that God is everywhere.
6. I said that I was reading a book.
7. He bade farewell to his friend.
8. I asked Sita if she would buy a new kurta.
9. Gopal asked me whether I played basketball.
10. Mohan said to Sohan where he lived.

While changing the direct into indirect speech changes need to be made in respect of tenses, pronouns, verbs and other words of the reported speech. In direct speech the actual words used by the speaker are placed within inverted commas; the reported speech is distanced from the reporting verb by a comma. The first word of the reported speech begins with a capital letter. Now let us consider the indirect speech – here no inverted commas are used. No comma is placed between reporting verb and the reported speech. The conjunction 'that' is generally used after the reporting verb. The verbs and the tense in the reported speech are changed.

Examples

Lata said, "Lakshmi works hard." (direct)

Lata said that Lakshmi worked hard. (indirect)

81. How should one use the following words?

affects, effects; but, butt; caste, cast; cost, cast; corps, corpse.

1. 'Affect' means influence and 'effect' means results (outcome).

Examples: The leader's image affects voters.

The effects of inflation will be seen in the budget.

2. 'But' means only.

'Butt' means target to ridicule; a large cask / barrel; short remnant; push with the head (as a verb).

Examples: Take my pen but return it immediately.

'Butt' used as target for ridicule; stub, short remnant.

Examples: Gita became a butt of laughter.

Kumar crushed the cigarette butt in the ashtray.

3. 'Caste' means a community.

Cast means list of actors.

Examples: Gopi and Radha belong to different castes and hence can't marry.

The cast of the new movie has not yet been decided.

4. Cost means price, cast means characters.

Examples: What is the cost of this soap?

The cost of sugar has gone up.

Have you decided the cost of the drama for the annual day?

Cast also means see direct (or) sideways (a glance).

Examples: Arun casts glances on every girl he passes by.

Kumar cast a glance at his new employee.

It is important to know that as a verb apart fro meaning direct (a glance), register (cast a vote), cas also means throw / shed. *Example:* The snake casts away its skin regularly. While using cast as a noun apart from meaning set of actors (in a play /drama) it also means type, quality.

5. Corps, corpse

'Corps' means division of an army

'Corpse' means a dead body

Examples

The corps have been called in to red alert areas.

The corpse was taken away for post mortem.

82. How are the articles 'a, an, the' used?

While using such articles one should be careful.

They are often misused as follows:

1. 'The' is used in the place of 'a'.
2. 'A' is omitted in the place it should be.
3. 'A' is used in the place it should not be.

Consider the word 'English'

When you use 'the' here, the meaning changes.

English refers to the language.

The English refers to *Englishmen*.

The mere inclusion of an article changes the meaning drastically.

Now let us consider the article 'a'. Look at the following sentences:

Examples

I saw a painter and a sculptor.

I saw a painter and sculptor.

In the first sentence it is *a painter* and *a sculptor* (here at two places 'a' is used) and in the second sentence it is a *painter and sculptor* (here the *a* with *sculptor* is gone). Now note the change in the meaning.

The first sentence implies having seen two person one is a painter and the other a sculptor.

In contrast the second sentence says having seen a person who is a painter and sculptor, (that is to say, only a single person was seen, who knows two art forms, painting and sculpture).

Therefore one should not use 'a, an, the' carelessly. Look at the following sentences:

1. The prime minister of India and the president of the congress party.
2. The chief minister of Tamil Nadu and General Seceratory of AIADMK party

The first sentence clearly implies that they are two persons (Manmohan Singh, Sonia Gandhi). In the second sentence it is clear that only one person (Miss Jayalalita) holds both the posts.

'a, an' are used together as a 'unit' and 'the' is used as a separate entity.

1. 'A, an' are used with countable nouns.
   a flower, a boy, a fruit, a book.
2. 'A, an' are used with singulars only.
   a flower.
3. 'A, an' are used in the instances of first time introduction.
   I saw a dog. The dog was chasing a boy. The boy was running for his life.

In these sentences usage of 'a' is done while first using (introducing) the words dog, boy. While using these words the second time 'the' is used: the dog, the boy. Therefore articles 'a, an', are used while using (introducing) a countable noun for the first time. One should always pronounce the articles 'a, an' properly.

a - | eI

an - | "en| or |"n|

the - |"

A is used before the singular nouns having the characteristics sound of the first syllable as in:

book – a book

table – a table

litre – a litre

horse – a horse

river – a river

watch – a watch

'An' is used before such singular nouns with the characteristics sound of the first syllable as in:

eye – an eye

ant – an ant

ink bottle – an ink bottle

umbrella – an umbrella

hour – an hour

MLA – an MLA

'A' is placed before the word *university*. Similarly in 'similar sounding first syllable' words (sound 'U') European 'unique' one rupee note all begin with 'a'.

a European

a unique book

a one rupee note

'A, an', are also used in some idioms and phrases.

Examples

a few, a little, many a, all of a sudden, ten rupee a day, a good deal of, a great deal of, 70 km an hour, a lot of, on an average, a piece of, a hundred, a shame, a pity.

Articles 'a, an, the' are also used before an adjective which comes before a noun.

Examples

He is a boy.

Shyam is a good boy.

Varun is an intelligent boy.

In the first sentence 'boy' is a singular countable noun with characteristically sounding first syllable. Here the boy is being talked about for the first time (introduction). Hence the usage 'a boy'.

In the second sentence the *adjective good* describes Shyam, following the adjective *good* comes the noun *boy* (singular, countable). Similarly in the third sentence the adjective *intelligent* is followed by the singular countable noun *boy*. Hence the article *a* is used – *a good boy*. *An* is used, *an intelligent boy*. A, an here are primarily due to the countable singular noun 'boy' because sentences two and three can also be written as:

Shyam is good.

Varun is intelligent.

(Here *a, an* are not used).

Other Books on

WORD POWER SERIES

1. Idiomatic English (How to Write & Speak It) **(New)** 175/-
2. School Essays, Letters, Applications, Paragraphs, and Stories For Higher Secondary Students **(New)** 110/-
3. Effective English Comprehension Read Fast, Understand Better! **(New)** 195/-
4. Latest Essays for College & Competitive Examinations **(New)** 150/-
5. Dictionary of New Words **(New)** 125/-
6. Art of English Conversation Speak English Fluently **(New)** 150/-
7. Teach Yourself English Grammar & Composition **(New)** 150/-
8. Common & Uncommon Proverbs **(New)** 160/-
9. Effective Editing : Help yourself in Becoming a Good Editor 150/-
10. Effective English A Boon for Learners **(New)** 125/-
11. Essays for Primary Classes 60/-
12. Essays for Junior Classes 60/-
13. Essays for Senior Classes 60/-
14. Dictionary of Synonyms and Antonyms 150/-
15. Dictionary of Idioms and Phrases 150/-
16. Common Phrases 150/-
17. How to Write & Speak Correct English 150/-
18. Meaningful Quotes 195/-
19. Punctuation Book 125/-
20. Top School Essays 125/-
21. How to Write Business Letters with CD 250/-
22. Everyday Grammar 160/-
23. Everyday Conversation 160/-
24. Letters for All Occasions 125/-
25. School Essays & Letters for Juniors 125/-
26. Common Mistakes in English 150/-
27. The Power of Writing 175/-
28. Learn English in 21 Lessons 150/-
29. First English Dictionary 125/-
30. Boost Your Spelling Power 150/-

31. Self-Help to English Conversation 150/-
32. The Art of Effective Communication 175/-
33. A Book of Proverbs & Quotations 125/-
34. Word Power Made Easy 160/-
35. English Grammar Easier Way 160/-
36. General English for Competitive Examinations 160/-
37. Spoken English 150/-
38. School Essays, Letters Writing and Phrases 125/-
39. How to Write & Speak Better English 150/-
40. Quote Unquote (A Handbook of Famous Quotations) 175/-
41. Improve Your Vocabulary 150/-
42. Common Errors in English 150/-
43. The Art of Effective Letter Writing 150/-
44. Synonyms & Antonyms 150/-
45. Idioms 150/-
46. Business Letters 125/-

Lotus PRESS

Unit No. 220, 2nd Floor, 4735/22, Prakash Deep Building,
Ansari Road, Darya Ganj, New Delhi- 110002
Ph.: 23280047, 9811594448
• E-mail : lotuspress1984@gmail.com, www.lotuspress.co.in